UNDERSTANDING SOCIETY, CULTURE, AND TELEVISION

UNDERSTANDING SOCIETY, CULTURE, AND TELEVISION

Paul Monaco

PRAEGER

Westport, Connecticut
London

Library of Congress Cataloging-in-Publication Data

Monaco, Paul.
    Understanding society, culture, and television / Paul Monaco.
        p. cm.
    Includes bibliographical references and index.
    ISBN 0–275–96057–9 (alk. paper)—ISBN 0–275–97095–7 (pbk.: alk. paper)
    1. Television broadcasting—Social aspects.   I. Title.
PN1992.6.M62   1998
302.23′.45—dc21   97–43945

British Library Cataloguing in Publication Data is available.

Library of Congress Catalog Card Number: 97–43945
ISBN: 0–275–97095–7 (pbk.)

First published in 1998

Praeger Publishers, 88 Post Road West, Westport, CT 06881
An imprint of Greenwood Publishing Group, Inc.
www.praeger.com

Printed in the United States of America

The paper used in this book complies with the
Permanent Paper Standard issued by the National
Information Standards Organization (Z39.48–1984).

10 9 8 7 6 5 4 3 2 1

Contents

Preface

All books originate somewhere and at a specific time. This one had its genesis during an afternoon's conversation with my friend Marty Seligman at his home just west of Philadelphia several summers ago. It was then that I decided to write a basic, readable book about television to clarify the nature of the medium and its relationship to society and culture.

The deeper sources that brought me to write this book were convoluted. For two-and-a-half decades, I have been exploring how the media arts of film and television both resemble and are different from the traditional arts. At the heart of this matter is the nature of art itself and its development during the course of the twentieth century. In recent years, I have also become increasingly interested in claims about media "effects" upon society and culture. I have been astonished to discover that so much that is believed about these so-called effects is so poorly reasoned.

Since that summer day when Marty and I had our long conversation, bipartisan congressional support passed the 1996 Telecommunications Act that was signed into law by President Bill Clinton. It mandates that V chips be installed in all new television sets sold in the United States so that certain programming can be blocked, and also requires a mandatory rating system for television programs. Underlying the Telecommunications Act are widespread myths about television, society, and culture that have been promoted for decades. While I see occasional glimpses of public and professional skepticism about these myths, they are nonetheless proving difficult to dislodge. As a step toward that goal, this book asks its readers to think through a welter of claims about television, society, and culture. In so doing, I have taken to task commonly held ideas about art, popular culture, technology, and the media and their "effects."

My understanding of television has benefitted enormously over the past several years from conversations that I have had with three of the medium's masters: the directors of episodes for several of TV's most popular programs, Jerome Courtland (*Dynasty*, *Falcon Crest*, and *Knot's Landing*) and Jeff Meyer (*Coach*, *Everybody Loves Raymond*, and *The Closer*), as well as the producer/writer for *Star Trek: Voyager*, Brannon Braga.

Throughout this book I acknowledge those many authors who have influenced me positively, as well as pointing out the other researchers and writers with whom I strongly disagree. No written comments, however, can adequately express my thanks to my wife Victoria O'Donnell. Her own writings on propaganda and persuasion, as well as in television criticism, are a continuing source of inspiration to me. In admiration, I dedicate this book to her.

1

Storytelling and Television

I went to college in New York City during the early 1960s. One of my best friends was a fellow student named Scott. He was an English major who liked to write and fancied himself to be a sort of beatnik poet. After graduating with his bachelor's degree he entered the advertising business and succeeded on Madison Avenue. By his mid-thirties, Scott was the president of a major agency. He was living in a grand apartment on Manhattan's upper east side and dating glamorous women. He had a weekend condo in Sag Harbor on the Long Island shore and afforded himself the best of everything.

Then, in 1978, I heard that he had given it all up. He resigned his position at the ad agency, completed the paperwork to pass his apartment on to an old girlfriend, bought a small used car and headed west. He was "dropping out" big time, disappearing with nary a trace. Several years later, I heard that he had wound up in the most remote and isolated part of Nevada, in a tiny hamlet with a gas station, a bar, and a handful of adobe houses. For a number of months he was able to live there off the cash he had taken with him when he left New York City. But his former lifestyle had not enabled him to save all that much and, in dropping out, he had closed his bank accounts and destroyed his credit cards.

This remote part of Nevada proved to be healing for Scott. He loved the openness of the place, its clean air and tranquility. He went to sleep hearing coyotes wail and awoke to the sounds of hawks as they soared at dawn. Recognizing that he would need some income to continue living this idyllic and simple life, he was delighted to hear one day that a bartender at the hamlet's saloon had quit. He applied for the job and got it from the owner, an elderly woman named Rose who owned the largest ranching operation within 300 miles. Rose liked Scott and trusted him from their first meeting. She gave him the bartending job on a single condition: if anyone ever came into the place and announced that "Savage Sam" was coming, Scott would clear the bar and close it immediately. He agreed.

For about a year everything was fine. Scott enjoyed his work. The atmosphere in the saloon was mellow and steady. His customers were nearly all old-timers, former cowhands and the like, whose stories he enjoyed. Late one afternoon, however, a bruised and bloodied man weakly pushed open the saloon's swinging doors, staggered to the middle of the room, muttered "Savage Sam is coming!" and collapsed. There were only three customers in the place. Two of them, seated at the bar, jumped up and ran out the swinging doors. The third, a loner who always drank at the small table next to the wood stove in the back of the room, leaped up and jumped out an open window. No problem clearing the place.

Before he could gather his wits, however, Scott glanced over to the swinging doors at the front of the saloon. A man on horseback had ridden up. Sitting atop his massive shoulders was a live bobcat. Scott began to tremble and hyperventilate. The man, who was seven-feet tall and rippling with muscles, grabbed each of the swinging doors at their tops and swung them open. As he did, he pulled the hinges off one of them. He strode to the bar, stopping directly across from Scott. The bobcat bared its fangs and hissed. This giant of a man looked over at the fellow who had collapsed on the floor and spat a wad of tobacco in his direction. He turned back to Scott, who was trembling and covered with sweat.

"Give me a drink," he yelled.

"Wha' . . . what do you want?"

"Whiskey!"

Scott turned; tears were welling in his eyes. Having grabbed a bottle of the bar's best bourbon, he steadied himself enough to take a shotglass in the other hand and returned to the bar. The giant of a man looked angry. The bobcat held on tighter to his shoulders and hissed again! Scott's hand was trembling so badly that he poured as much whiskey on the bar as he did in the shotglass. When it was full the stranger grabbed it and swallowed the drink.

"Give me another."

But before Scott could pour it, the man reached over and grabbed the bottle out of his hand. He pulled off the pouring spout, threw it aside, and began to drink directly from the bottle. He stepped back from the bar as he did. The bobcat hissed again and flailed its paw in the air. The man drank in loud, steady gulps. Scott closed his eyes; tears were running down his cheeks and onto his shirt, which was sticking to his skin now because he was covered with so much perspiration. He opened his eyes at the sound of the bottle crashing on the floor when the man threw it down after finishing the last drops.

Turning away from the bar, the stranger belched, looked quickly around the saloon, spat again, and in the same motion drew a hundred dollar bill from his shirt pocket and threw it on the bar. Scott was frozen in his spot. The stranger turned and headed toward the door. Scott watched him. Then, lunging forward, he picked up the hundred dollar bill from the wet bar, and called out, "Wait! That bottle of bourbon only costs eighty dollars; you've got change coming."

The stranger was nearly to the door, when he turned his head: "Change? I ain't got time! Gotta get goin'. Ain't you heard? Savage Sam is comin'!"

Put simply, the structure of the Savage Sam story can be summarized:

1.   In college one of my best friends was a fellow student named Scott.

This is a statement that the reader (viewer/listener) is likely to take at face value. It is to be assumed that what is coming next is a personal recollection. You might be led to think that the story about to unfold took place while both Scott and I were in college or that it is about something that I witnessed firsthand. Actually the story is about neither. My claimed connection to Scott turns out to be inconsequential. It is like a "teaser" or a "hook" at the beginning of an episodic drama or a sitcom on TV. Watch how, in the first minute and a half or two, before the first set of commercials on nearly any television episode, a scene is presented that is intended to draw in the viewer and to dramatically pose the question as to where the story is headed.

2.   After the tease, the second part of the story describes success, wealth, and

possible happiness: the life of an up-and-comer in a New York ad agency living in the fast lane.

3. Scott abruptly leaves New York City for Nevada. Little is told as to why he does this, or how he came to that decision. In the story, there is no detailed inner revelation of his thoughts and feelings behind this departure.
4. For a while he leads an idyllic and peaceful life in the hamlet in Nevada, but he needs money to keep living there.
5. He gets a job as a bartender on the single condition that he'll clear the bar and close it if he ever hears that Savage Sam is coming.
6. One day a battered and bruised man comes in and collapses and the bar clears; another giant of a man, with a bobcat on his shoulders, comes in and demands a drink.
7. Punch line!

Only items five and six are absolutely necessary for the joke to work. The rest of the story consists of elements and details that could be changed or omitted. Individual segments of this story, for example items two, three, and four, might each be taken as the premise for three different and complete seasons of a TV series. In such an instance, each of the situations provides an "arc" or trajectory through which a character passes. Item five could provide the premise for a complete season also. Item six, however, is not a premise but an action, and item seven provides a resolution.

From the story of Savage Sam, which is based on a joke told to me many years ago, we could plausibly have sufficient material to form the kernel of an idea from which to produce a TV series lasting several seasons. The series would be held together from season to season by the central character Scott. During each season the arc would present him with different problems: for example, item two, working with colleagues at the agency; satisfying clients and keeping them happy; moving up the ladder; becoming president of the agency; item three, living in the fast lane; going in and out of romantic relationships; holding things down at the agency; deciding to buy a condo in Sag Harbor and not somewhere else. Optionally there may even be enough here for yet another season, namely item three-and-a-half. This would be based upon Scott becoming disillusioned with the advertising business and life in the city; finding the people around him to be shallow; discovering that he wants something else in life; item four, Scott's initial experiences and adventures in desolate Nevada; the folk of the hamlet and its surrounding area; seeing his money run out; getting the bartending job at the saloon; item five, his life as the bartender; old-timers and their tales; a romance with a young woman who works on a ranch near the saloon; an episode with the city slickers who get lost and drop in; the Savage Sam resolution.

The premises on which episodic television are based, and also the scripts that are written for such series from week to week, are highly formulaic. They follow common patterns. Many people believe that because they can see through these formulas that they can write such scripts themselves. It may look simple, but it isn't! Only a small percentage of the people who try writing scripts ever succeed in seeing them produced. Of those who do have scripts produced, an even smaller number are able to sustain media writing careers. Television scripts are less like traditional literature than they are like blueprints for building houses. They are subject to constant rewrites and changes. In writing for television, teams of writers, perhaps up to as many as twenty for a prime-time sitcom or drama, may toil together to grind out a single episode. Or else members of the writing team may take turns writing specific episodes which are then pulled apart and reconstructed.

In the movies and in television the unit costs of production are high, ranging from one to two million dollars for a typical half-hour TV episode (which actually is just twenty-one or twenty-two minutes long to accommodate the commercials) and forty to seventy-five million dollars for a feature film for the big screen. Therefore, it is vital for the storytellers in these media to try to build in a substantial degree of predictability in order to hedge against the high financial risks of these projects. This is done by finding characters and situations that hold up well over time. But such familiarity and repetition must be kept alive by having the writers come up with inventive shifts and subtleties that push the formula in slightly different, and sometimes unexpected, directions.

Stories on episodic television, much like the tale of Savage Sam, can be picked up and followed even if a listener/viewer misses a significant portion of what has come before. Television's patterns of repetition emphatically reinforce this by the fact that programs are packaged in series. Viewers know from week to week who the central character(s) is (are), what the relationships are between the characters, and where the action is taking place. When it comes to TV, familiarity breeds contentment, not contempt. We can tune in, be distracted, come back, and, when worse comes to worse and our viewing of an episode is disrupted entirely, know that in the same place at the same time a new episode will be back again next week.

Primarily, TV is about story telling. In general, effective stories are based on the tensions created between opposing forces. Court cases, either criminal or civil, provide great story material. They are based upon adversarial relationships, between the state and the accused, between a plaintiff and a defendant, or between a victim and the accused. Much of what goes on in society that becomes newsworthy can be presented as involving tensions between individuals, political parties, races, special interests, social classes, or nations.

Some degree of conflict or tension is necessary for any good story line. Stories are at their best for television when they are highly accessible, easily understood, fall within a range of plausibility, and strike viewers as familiar enough to fit easily into patterns of repetition. The differences between effective stories for television tend to be small and subtle. Their appeal is in the comfort of familiarity they provide, not in their ability to uproot or to shock us. They succeed in direct proportion to large numbers of people becoming accustomed to them. They are best liked and most admired precisely in those instances in which a familiar formula is taken and modified slightly.

In everyday English "telling stories" means fabricating fibs or white lies. But a story, as a story, is neither good nor bad in a moral sense. Narrative structure is simply a way of ordering experience in a compelling and dramatic manner. Telling something as a story potentially makes it become engaging. Mastery over its narrative elements makes the telling of a story more entertaining, a word, by the way, having roots in the Latin *entare* meaning to hold. Instead of telling the Savage Sam story at the beginning of this chapter, I might have just stated its central idea in one line: "Things aren't always what they seem to be." The value of a story is in its telling, and that telling is elaborated and embellished in the nuances, the twists, and the turns of any particular rendition of any specific tale.

It is astonishing how literal-minded and inaccurate so much criticism of television has become. Donella H. Meadows of Dartmouth College advances this claim: "Have you ever looked at the script of a TV show, even a news show, even a sober PBS documentary? There is no logical flow. The words are there as commentary on the pictures. The pictures are chosen not to build up a sequence of thought, but to engage the emotions. Sustained intelligence is hard enough in a visual medium even if that were the intent of the producers which it rarely is."[1]

Let us say, however, that we are producing the Savage Sam story as a video to air on television. As written, the story begins with a reference to my having known Scott in college. We might show pictures of a bucolic small town campus, although that is inaccurate because the written version begins: "I went to college in New York City." So, alternatively we may elect not to show the viewer anything that places the campus in its geographic context. We might just show a group of undergraduate men and women in a dining hall. We might show a crowd of student-aged people huddled together in the bleachers at a football game. We might show someone studying alone in the library. We might show a graduation ceremony. And so on. Some pictures fit, while others don't! If we show the launch of Apollo 13 from Cape Canaveral, or if we show wolves foraging in the woods, or if we show the Frugal Gourmet preparing a souffle, or if we show a tankful of tropical fish, then none of these pictures fit the script information: "In college, I knew a fellow student named Scott."

The pictorial content that we choose, and how we go about filming or taping it, has everything to do with the logic of what the audience sees and hears. Do we begin with a long shot, looking down from a high vantage point, of Scott as a tiny figure crossing an empty campus on a gray and misty morning? Do we begin with a close-up of his face as he studies intently in the library, with the camera pulling out from him to reveal a softly lit and muted ambiance? Do we start with a medium shot of him in the midst of a boozy bunch of fellow students cheering at a football game being played on a sunny afternoon?

The content of each of these shots conveys information. Elements such as the lighting, the colors, and their contrasts convey mood. The length of each shot conveys intent. A twenty-second shot of Scott walking across an empty campus carries a different value than if it were only five seconds long. The angle of the camera and its focal length from the subject, the lighting, and the action that occurs within the frame are all choices. They are hardly arbitrary, capricious, illogical, or meaningless, as critics like Donella Meadows claim.

In a different story, the visual choices would be different. If the voice opens, "In college, I knew a fellow student named Scott," and we see waves rolling in on the shore, then the voice-over may next say: "I really got to know Scott that weekend that four of us went to Cape Cod in April of our senior year." Or the voice might say: "Scott loved the ocean. He talked about it all the time and wrote poems about the sea that he'd read to us late at night in the dorm." Pictures are not arbitrary.

Nearly any viewer would question the choice of beginning the Savage Sam story with shots of the ocean, so long as the story is told on film or tape just as I presented it at the beginning of this chapter.

Just what does Donella Meadows mean when she claims that there is no "logical flow" in television? Television, as a system of communication, is linear and progressive. It proceeds by accretion, building from one program to the next, from one season to the next, from one series (which may last a number of seasons) to the next. Television depends upon subtle shifts and adjustments. Those who balk at terms such as infotainment shudder to think that the news or documentaries rely upon storytelling techniques and dramatization. But why? That something is factual or reality based in no way interferes with the necessity to order its telling into a narrative form.

In one of the lectures in the introductory course that I teach, I describe the following situation. Let us say that before the class session began, I had set up five video cameras in the room. One is hanging from the ceiling in a back corner. In the other back corner, I have placed a camera on a tripod so it's elevated six feet above the floor. A third camera is placed just eighteen inches above the floor, near the front of the room and is angled upward with the lens pointing at the students. In the other front corner a camera is mounted near the ceiling, angling downward. The fifth camera is placed on the wall just behind the spot from which I lecture. It is set at a height of six feet, and tilted only slightly toward the students' seats. I've selected the positions and angles of each camera. Additionally, I have equipped a couple of them so that they will move mechanically, either tilting up and down slowly, or panning left to right and back again. As soon as the class begins, I activate all the cameras so that they begin recording. The class period is fifty minutes long. When the class is over, I turn the cameras off.

From my five different cameras I have 250 minutes of videotape, which is more than four hours worth. I review all my tapes. Some of the footage is awful. Some of it is fine. The camera may have caught a student's expression that is especially appealing, or it has captured me leaning in toward the group and gesturing in an animated manner. The 250 minutes of tape is, in its raw stages, not a film, not a video, not a program! But, it *can* be shaped into one.

I then edit all this tape, ending up with a ten minute finished production entitled *Classroom*. What shots I consider to be best for inclusion in the final version are determined by several criteria. Those visuals that have good technical qualities of composition and lighting may be kept for that reason alone. More importantly, shots displaying the appropriate human content, or information, will be selected. Most importantly, the choice of shots is driven by the point of view being expressed. If *Classroom* is a serious piece, meant to convey that something meaningful and valuable is occurring in the class, different shots and sound will be selected than if it is meant to be comic. If the intent is humor, facial expressions will be picked that seem funny, and the sound will be cut with them to create a feeling of lightheartedness or satire. If it is serious, we will select the pictures of students with serious demeanor and focused expressions. We will have to leave out the shots of students yawning or rolling their eyes in disbelief and boredom.

The final production depends upon which shots are chosen, how they are arranged, and how long each stays on the screen. The sound content of this edited and finished version may be matched to my voice as I actually taught the class. Or, in editing, we can take a voice segment and mismatch it to pictures of student reactions that actually occurred at another point in time. Or, we may elect to record other sound after the class, such as student reactions to the instructor and comments about him, which then may be edited into the final tape. Alternatively, I may write a separate voice-over script, record it, and match it to the pictures on the tape in order to give the finished production yet another point of view. In film and video, editing is every bit the equal of writing for purposes of the final scripting of a production. We should never be naive about the complex ways in which picture and sound may be woven together in movies, video, and TV, nor should we ever misjudge television by claiming it to be exclusively a visual medium.

Think for a moment about a television program on the reintroduction of the wolf to Yellowstone National Park. The opening scene shows wolves roaming across a snowy field; cut to a park ranger addressing a group of tourists in a presentational meeting at the Old Faithful Lodge, where she is describing the feeding habits of wolves; cut to a hearing in the United States Senate where a witness is being questioned about the alleged threat of wolves to domestic livestock when they venture outside the park boundaries. The sequence consists of three discrete scenes that are not necessarily or inherently connected. This is because the logic of the media arts, although consistent within its own terms, is not determined by a preexisting structure. In this sense, television or film is not limited in the way that language is. While many of the most highly respected theorists have argued that film is a language, I find this idea to be helpful only marginally and metaphorically. Analytically, emphasis should be on how these media are *not* language. If I say, "Go me home after work," the listener will understand what I mean. But unless I am perceived as trying to be poetic, the listener concludes that my statement constitutes incorrect usage and a violation of English grammar. There are no such rules in film/television, although there are conventions. These conventions are based upon assumptions about what will be easiest and most comfortable for the average viewer's eye and ear to follow.

The producers of the video on wolves in Yellowstone look for ways to smooth the transition from sequence to sequence, either in picture or sound.   Take, for example, the three segments described above. Transitions between them might be made visually. The tape could cut from the wolves sniffing in the snow to the same image being shown on a screen during the ranger's presentation, with the camera then pulling out to reveal visually where she is and to whom she is talking. There might be a dissolve from a closeup of the ranger's face at the end of this sequence to the face of a female scientist speaking, with the camera then pulling out from her close-up to reveal that she is testifying in a Senate hearing; or, there may be a cut from her to a shot of the faces of inquisitive lawmakers. If the producer of the tape elects not to edit the piece in some manner that attempts to match the images visually, he or she may rely on continuing background music through all three of the segments for continuity.

Many critics of television maintain that informational TV programming trivializes ideas by sacrificing content to personality. Everyone wants to be able say that content should never be sacrificed to personality! Upon closer examination, however, just what does this mean? The writings of Karl Marx are seminal to socialist theory; those of Sigmund Freud to psychoanalysis; those of Friedrich Nietzsche to a critique of traditional moral systems and the origins of existentialism. We do not need to be obsessed with the biographies of these thinkers to understand that the shape of their thoughts had something to do with when they lived and wrote and also had something to do with their personalities. Who they were had much to do with how they arrived at their formulations, why they coined particular phrases, and why their writing emphasized certain points and not others. All thought is *someone's* thought. It does not matter necessarily through which medium we experience an idea. If we read a pathbreaking book and then hear a live lecture by the author, we may conclude that he or she is a better writer than a speaker, or the opposite! Such perceptions, however, do not determine ideas.

Just now, as I was writing about the sample documentary on wolves in Yellowstone National Park, I thought that I might wish to quote a passage from Arthur Koestler's 1938 novel *Darkness at Noon*. I got up from the computer and went over to my bookshelves to look for my copy. As I was searching, the following flashed through my mind.

1. I recalled first reading the novel during my eighteenth summer when the weather was very hot in Albany, New York, and doing so evenings under a shady tree in Washington Park.
2. I remembered a professor of intellectual history at Columbia University who taught the novel and revealed to me an exciting context in which to appreciate it. This led to my thinking about assigning and teaching the same novel myself in Dallas, at the University of Texas.

In some frustration at not finding the book, I started thinking:

3. my copy was at home in our house in Gallatin Gateway, Montana, which associated
4. to the home in which I was raised in Albany, New York.

Still not finding my copy of *Darkness at Noon*, I wondered about:

5. why I misplace things, and
6. the sloppiness of habit and mind I associate with so doing, and
7. my very negative judgment of such behavior.

Concluding that I should still be able to find my copy, I recalled

8. the last time I remembered using the book, which was when I was preparing a video installation on Berlin several years earlier,
9. which was presented subsequently at an art museum in Portland, Oregon,
10. reminding me of my last time in that city, an event entirely unrelated to the museum show, when I ate great crab cakes at Jake's, an old seafood restaurant where my wife, Victoria, ordered a single-malt scotch before dinner that cost twelve dollars per shot.

At this point, I decided

11. that I could easily get a copy of *Darkness at Noon* at the university's library

if I could not find my own copy,

12. reflecting upon how the department's regular secretary, who is on leave right now, is always so good at helping me find misplaced items.

I returned to my computer!

This gamut of thoughts, a dozen distinct and different ones as I choose to number them and the process of association that connects them, describes one form of mental process. When I returned to my writing, my mind was more focused and linear for some time, although not to the exclusion of all extraneous and associated thoughts.

Mental process always combines focus and randomness, concentration and free association, earnestness and frivolity. So do the various media. Most of television proceeds in a linear, progressive way. Some television is random and disjointed. A nature documentary does "think" differently than an MTV music video. And a "pop-up" music video, with bubble-text commentaries edited into the original, thinks differently than a conventional music video that lacks such additional text. But the way something thinks does not necessarily determine the way *we* think in response to it! We are neither the books we read, nor the television programs we watch, nor the paintings we hang on our walls. To assume so ignores all the myriad individual acts of translation and transformation that must process everything that we encounter, no matter through what medium it is presented to us.

Media stories are highly stylized and repetitive. They lack the power of those traditional cultural stories that are labeled myths. Movie screens and television sets are not oracles from which agreed-upon truths emanate. The stories of the movies and TV are non empowered. They are contrivances like the Savage Sam story that I recounted at the beginning of the chapter. In the late twentieth century, however, various theorists promote the false view that all stories are woven into society and culture in fundamentally the same way. But the story of Christ, for example, is *entirely* different from the Savage Sam story. Any story that is understood as a philosophic, religious, or patriotic truth differs from one that is understood as a diversion and amusement. Still, academic rhetoric fuels widespread doggerel claiming that all stories are central to the belief systems of their listeners/viewers, which is at the very heart of the popular idea that the media arts are capable of a bewildering set of effects that influence their audiences. Tales are truth, however, only in social circumstances where they are made to be so. Pluralistic democracies do not provide the basis for the sharing of stories as systems of belief in the manner that communitarian societies do.

Art is the conscious and purposeful manipulation of formal elements of expression into form. Art has nothing inherently to do with beauty and inspiration. The sunset I may see driving home in the evening is beautiful and inspirational, but it occurs in nature and therefore is not art. Art must always be human made, and, in that sense, is always artificial. The television series *Beavis and Butt-head* is art, even though I may find it neither beautiful nor inspirational. The telling of contrived stories is a central element of television art. The art of television, however, must be understood more broadly, for it is not just storytelling.

NOTE

1. Donella H. Meadows, "We Are What We Watch," in *The Baltimore Sun*, September 28, 1994. Originally written for *The Los Angeles Times*.

2

Television and the Aesthetics of Power, Virtuosity, and Repetition

An answer to the question, "What kind of an art form is television?" is not arrived at easily. To begin exploring that question, however, think first about entering a gallery or a museum where either paintings or still photographs are exhibited. As you enter, you look around the space and approach a work hanging on the wall to the left just inside the door. You pause in front of it for twenty-five to thirty seconds. Then you move to the work on its right. This next piece does little for you; you gaze at it for several seconds and move on. You continue down the row until you come upon a painting you like a lot. You stay awhile in front of it, balancing yourself alternately on the left or right foot. You are moved by his work and your body shows it! You step forward so that you can look at the details. You shuffle back several steps to take it in from a longer distance. Then you recall something that you saw in the first work that you looked at. You cross the room quickly, looking at it again with new eyes.

This is not the case with film, video, and television. Nor is it true with going to the theatre or listening to music. How our time is controlled in experiencing each of these art forms depends upon the creative decisions of those who produce or perform the work. If you own a videotape, somewhere on its case or package you will find its length. If it is one hour and thirty-two minutes, then whenever it is played at normal speed it will consistently last ninety-two minutes. The videocassette player permits us to stop a video if the phone rings or to rewind the tape if we would like to watch a scene a second time. But this constitutes only a curiosity permitted by technology that has nothing to do with the art form itself. Any movie or video is created out of distinct temporal segments, the exact length of which is determined by the makers.

A painter, a photographer, an architect, or a writer makes assumptions about how long a typical viewer or reader may spend with his or her work and may even attempt to guide that engagement, but he or she has no real control over it. The absolute temporal control exerted by the makers of film, video, and TV over their art suggests that these media may have a similar kind of control over audiences. This observation provokes the idea that the maker's control over time in film, video, and TV means that these media are exceptionally manipulative of viewers. This notion, however, is vague and contradicts everyday observations about the differences between movies and television and how we watch them.

Movies hold their audiences well. They do so, however, because of structural factors pertaining to where and how they are seen. When we go to a movie theater, we pay directly to see a particular film at a specific showing. Unless we find a movie extraordinarily offensive or unsatisfactory, we are likely to stay for the entire show. The moviegoer's patience is based upon having left home and having paid for transportation and/or parking. The moviegoer may also be dining out either before or after the show, hiring a baby-sitter for the evening, and arranging to meet friends, all of which are factors that substantially increase the investment in movie going as an event. Under these circumstances, staying with the movie usually makes good sense.

Television watchers are in an opposite position to moviegoers. They may be seeing something very much like a movie, if not the actual telecast of a film, but their behavior is markedly impatient. They are aided in acting on this impatience by the increasing number of channels available (broadcast, cable, or satellite) and by the remote control that makes the instantaneous changing of these channels effortless. Although movies and television commonly are linked, our viewing behaviors toward them are contradictory, although this contradiction has to do primarily with social and economic factors pertaining to movie going or watching TV.

Film as projected in a movie theater obviously differs greatly from watching a TV broadcast or a videocassette on a home monitor with the markedly poor visual and audio quality of most sets. But is this difference truly important? The fact is that millions of viewers can enjoy a movie on a television screen just as well as they can enjoy it in a theater. No matter how good or poor the quality of the picture and the sound, movies and television still share basic elements of storytelling and the ability to manipulate time and space. Think, for example, of the following sequence:

SHOT # 1 - An alarm clock on a small table rings; a male hand reaches into the frame to shut it off.

SHOT # 2 - A middle-aged man getting out of bed, stepping to the window where he draws open the curtain; view out the window is of distinguishable New York City (Manhattan) skyline.

SHOT # 3 - A cutaway to an open, nearly packed suitcase on the floor.

SHOT # 4 - The same man exiting the doorway of an apartment building, with suitcase in hand, and stepping off the curb and into the street.

SHOT # 5 - The man, in the backseat of a taxicab; vehicle passes sign reading "John F. Kennedy International Airport."

SHOT # 6 - A plane descending against a background of clear, blue sky; sets down on a runway; taxis left to right across the screen as the camera pans with it, revealing in the background the outline of the Eiffel Tower at a considerable distance.

SHOT # 7 - The same man, dressed differently, seated at a sidewalk café along a distinctively Parisian boulevard.

SHOT # 8 - An elegantly dressed woman enters the shot; they greet as if they know each other and he was expecting her; the man pulls back a chair so that she may sit; he summons the waiter.

This series of shots is commonplace. Nearly everyone on the globe understands this sequence and has no problem with the transitions of time and space in it. Each of the eight shots might be on the screen for ten seconds, making the entire sequence one minute, twenty seconds long. The sequence could be shortened by changing the length of specific shots, or by dropping a couple of them altogether. More likely it would be lengthened to add detail and to further develop its sense of drama or tension. Film, video, and television manipulate time and space easily and they do so with photographic precision. Each shot is a given in terms of the visual details contained in the frame. Writing out the same sequence in prose might read like this:

He awoke startled and turned off the alarm clock on the night table. He swung his weight across the bed, stepped down out of it and went to the window. The drapes opened upon a cloudless sky, which was rare in Manhattan. The facades of large apartment buildings and commercial skyscrapers glistened in the morning sunlight. He turned away from the window, glancing at his open, nearly packed suitcase on the floor.

As he left his apartment building, striding across the busy sidewalk, with a single gesture he stepped off the curb and raised his right hand, hailing a cab. The ride to Kennedy Airport was brief and uneventful. The cab driver, Iranian as he guessed from the name on his license displayed prominently on the visor, never spoke. Traffic was light; much less than he would have expected normally at this time on a weekday morning.

He slept for most of the flight, being awakened by an attendant only shortly before beginning the descent into Charles DeGaulle Airport. As the plane taxied to the gate, he caught a glimpse of the outline of the Eiffel Tower against the horizon at a great distance.

He felt surprisingly rested and alert. Making the trip across the Atlantic during the day was practically a joy compared to those overnight flights that left New York in the evening. He had checked in at his hotel, changed clothes and then walked to the Café de Flor on the Boulevard Saint Germaine. He had been seated only a few minutes when she appeared. Tall and graceful, wearing a flower-print dress, just as he remembered her. He stood up, pulled a chair out from the table for her, and sat back down himself after she did. Smiling at her, he summoned the waiter.

Reading this you may be imagining visual images of the persons or places described. If you have been to New York City or to Paris the images which come to your mind's eye are likelier to be more detailed and accurate than if you have not. In the last paragraph of the prose rendition the words "just as he remembered her," convey the information that they have not seen each other for some time. In the movie/video/TV scene this would have to be suggested by facial expressions and body language if there were no dialogue between them that made this point clear. Certain effects are stronger or easier to achieve in certain media. How, for example, would you stage this same sequence in a live theatrical presentation? This question might be answered in several different ways. At the most fundamental level, however, the question itself points out the fact that a stage, no matter how large, always confronts us with severe challenges in manipulating time and space. By contrast, a movie or a television screen, no matter how small, poses few challenges, if any, in this regard.

By its nature, all art is intended to draw in the viewer, reader, or listener effectively. The devices relied upon by the creator vary by medium and by his or her assessment of the potential audience for the work. The movies and television cast a broad net to gain mass audiences, but a performance artist playing to a house of twenty devotees is just as interested in holding that audience. Internally all works of art, whether they are representational or decorative, didactic or abstract, conventional or avant-garde, are intended to engage the viewer, reader, or listener at a level deemed sufficient by the maker to adequately support the work financially and critically. There is no inherent contradiction between art and entertainment, and it is among the more feeble intellectual conceits of our age to maintain that there is. Are movies, video, and television manipulative of their audiences? The response must be that, yes, of course they are, *internally*!

At the heart of what we really want to know about television are general questions pertaining to what art is and what it does. In essence, all art appeals to three different aspects of human sensibility: *power; virtuosity; repetition.*[1] Architecture, for example, most frequently produces works of power in whose sheer magnitude resides their appeal: the Egyptian pyramids of Gizah, the cathedrals of western Europe (such as Chartres or Cologne), the monuments to Washington, Jefferson, and Lincoln in Washington, D.C., the Taj Mahal, the Moscow subway, and the skyscrapers of North American cities. In the presence of these edifices, the viewer is bid to appreciate their dimensions and proportions, and to be taken in by their structural size and enormity of presence in physical space.

Power, however, does not necessarily have to be contingent upon size, mass, and proportion. Exceptions exist in any culture in which magic or the notion of an immediate and awesome transformation prevails. In the Roman Catholic mass, when the communion host and chalice are raised, devotional language is used, and bread and wine literally transformed into the body and blood of Christ, a transcendent power is invoked. It should not offend a believing Catholic to describe what occurs in this instance as the practice of a particular aesthetic idea. It is a fine example of the physical object of power actually being quite small. For a secular example, conjure up the image of a lapel pin in the form of an American flag, which is intended to invoke the same sense of history, honor, and pride that might be associated with a flag that is physically much larger.

The notion of virtuosity practically defines the modern concept of art in the Western world. Since the Renaissance of the fourteenth century, this idea has become interwoven with a strong cultural sense of individualism and personal autonomy. Around this idea Western culture has constructed a complex view of art and the artist's relationship to its making. We commonly believe that the artist is set apart as a striving individual who is driven to creativity over and against great odds: the artist struggling against repressive authority; the artist battling physical deformity or pain; the artist contending with his or her own abuse of alcohol or drugs; the artist in conflict with benighted patrons or audiences; the artist plagued by existential longing and angst. These struggles have been forged into legends in the biographies of artists. And this notion of struggle has been made pivotal in an ethos of artistic creativity that is still pervasive today. From such views come the abiding idea that art is the creation of an inspired individual vision and unique sensibility.

In the Western world this notion has further permeated the performing arts through the manner in which music and theatre have been become professions with their works scheduled and presented in specific places at specific times. It is writing, however, that constitutes the ultimate in virtuosity. Authorship subsumes the idea of a single creative sensitivity meeting that of another individual, the reader, at the juncture of the written page. An aesthetic of virtuosity celebrates and promotes the individual, the unique, and the distinctive.

As an artistic idea, virtuosity reached its high point in modernism, where the artist's ability to make manifest and express in a specific work personal feelings and inner perceptions becomes paramount. But, chronologically, just as the idea of artistic virtuosity and authorship was reaching its peak at the end of the nineteenth century, the motion pictures were invented, being first shown publicly in 1895. The movies departed from photography by causing a series of pictures to move through a projector at such a rate so as to give the impression of normal lifelike motion. The collaborative making of movies also marked a transition from the individual artistic work of the photographer. By the end of the First World War, film production meant making fictional movies, normally one-and-a-half to two hours long, in an industrial structure consisting of a rigid division of labor and an assembly line process. Virtuosity resided in the specific technical skills mastered by individual collaborators on a project, but the identities of these technicians were entirely secondary to the finished movie. Their art was to be celebrated only by the most diehard fans and in specialized forms of industry recognition such as the Academy Awards.

By traditional theatrical standards even the virtuosity of movie actors and actresses was called into question. How talented they were was answered commercially by the star system but not at a level that satisfied the other issues posed by that question. The movies are more than a century old, yet it remains unresolved as to how to assess the talent of screen performers. Are the most successful among them simply photogenic or is screen presence more complex? How does screen playing compare to live stage acting? The virtuosity of memorizing lines, timing, and blocking for a live stage performance is compromised in film by the repeatable nature of the fundamental unit in the production process, the *take*. Not only are movie performers given numerous attempts to get it right, but also voices can be dubbed in, the soundtrack sweetened, and doubles or stand-ins used for a variety of scenes including those in which the action may be the most daring and impressive.

The movies, and subsequently television, have relied most heavily upon patterns of repetitious appeal. Movies and television programs conform notably to *genre* and *type*, although the way repetition works in them means that new shows do not imitate their predecessors slavishly. Indeed, it is precisely because each new movie or TV program is just a little different from the last that the appearance of holding onto the aesthetic of virtuosity is maintained in them. It could be argued that the aesthetic of repetition that is so prominent in the movies and television replicates basic appeals found in traditional folk art and ritual. In these forms individual artistic creativity is subsumed by the expectation that what is presented will be faithful to an established pattern. The satisfaction provided by such works or performances depends upon the capacity of a craftsperson or a performer to faithfully reproduce rituals, dances, songs, images, shapes, patterns, and stories. Innovation initiated by the artist or performer is not desired. The votive figure is to be carved the next time just as it has been carved many times before. A ritual derives its meaning and value from its strict imitation of prior performances. Going back to the example of the Roman Catholic mass, the congregation will not applaud a priest who alters the communion rite; his virtuosity must be limited to the sermon that stands apart from the ritual itself.

At the dawn of the twenty-first century, repetition as an artistic value is popular and democratic. It works well for societies in which constantly growing numbers of people seek affordable pleasures and diversions that can be made easily and inexpensively available to them. And the movies and television can only be understood on a premise that proceeds from this fundamental recognition.

Power did function through the magic of the movies in the medium's earliest years.[2] The filmmaker's capacity to change time and space instantaneously, however, has lost its power over time as audiences have become accustomed to the movies. Power surely remains where the screen is big and the sound system dominating, as in one of the better upscale movie theaters. (An IMAX theater is an extreme example of this!) But in terms of the normal presentation of movies in theaters, the magic in the movies today resides primarily in the visuals of special effects that are limited to only certain productions. The medium's power to manipulate time and space no longer dazzles viewers.

Since the 1950s, moreover, the movies have flirted self-consciously with the idea of artistic virtuosity. This flirtation began just as the Hollywood studio system of production started to unravel. At the same time, the European art film appeared and a new critical theory toward the movies was being nurtured in France. The *auteur* theory advanced the idea that the director of a film is the single dominant artistic force behind its creation.[3] Predictably, this idea drew favorable attention in academic circles. More interestingly, over time it has attracted a strong degree of popular enthusiasm. In spite of its popularity, however, this "author" idea of movie making remains inherently problematic for a medium in which creativity is always collaborative. It is uncertain that any film director's style ever can be identifiable in a manner akin to the distinctive style of a painter or a writer. Walking in upon any movie at midpoint, you would be unlikely to recognize a specific director's work in the way that you might recognize an unfamiliar Picasso or Degas upon entering a museum.

Nonetheless, this *auteur* idea has meant that increasingly film directors have become individually well known. Moreover, in the business of producing movies, individual directors who make box office successes increasingly have been able to purchase greater indulgence of their artistic vision when contracting to direct new movies. Still, filmmaking remains a collaborative process that continues to be driven by the high unit cost of making a movie and by the producers' and directors' dependence upon an array of supporting artists, technicians, and other professionals. Interestingly, although television has everywhere become far more pervasive than the movies, few of us would know or recognize the names of any television directors. Television has resisted the idea of directorial virtuosity, although a few producers such as Aaron

Spelling, Steven Bochco, and Chris Carter have gained some fame. Neither critics nor the general public associate specific shows on television with the creative impulses and genius of their directors. In many ways the high pressure production practices in television are even more demanding than in movie making. That fact, however, remains a matter of indifference to both critics and the public when they evaluate such work.

Since the picture and sound of the average television set is so poor, the viewer likely attaches little sense of power to the medium's visual and audio presentation. A sense of power invariably depends, moreover, on where, when, and how something is presented. The TV set's presence in our midst as a home appliance works against any such sense of power. We stay at home to see and hear TV, and it is presented to us in a lit, or partially lit, portion of our dwelling. We are not surrounded by a public when we watch it. We even make only half hearted and incomplete efforts to avoid interruptions in our televiewing. Television has its origins as much in broadcast radio as it does in the motion pictures. You can listen to TV without watching it, and a lot of people do just that. The way in which we use TV at home means that we can be distracted from the screen or go about other things in our living space without completely diverting our attention away from the program. Television simplifies the visual range of the motion pictures. And because TV's art consists of repetition in the extreme, a large part of how television functions has to do with the establishment of viewer familiarity with characters, settings, situations, formats, and expectations from show to show.

Compared to film, indeed compared to *any* other medium, television has dramatically extended the idea of repetition everywhere in the world. Programs repeat daily. Entire time slots are predictably designated for news, talk shows, or soap operas. Episodic drama and sitcoms, which are the staple of prime-time TV, recur with weekly regularity the same day of the week and at a precise hour. Game shows appear daily or nightly in their specific time slots. When enough episodes are completed, usually at least a hundred, and it is perceived that a sufficiently large audience will watch the reruns, a TV program goes into syndication and what was once a weekly series will run nightly. And with specialized niche channels, such as CNN or MTV, news or music videos repeat constantly in a continuous pattern.

During the 1950s, the cultural critic Dwight Macdonald argued for a concept distinguishing so-called high art from popular art that doggedly continues to plague our understanding of television today. The works of high culture, Macdonald argued, are characterized by "an artist communicating his *individual* vision to other individuals." The popular arts such as television were to be lumped together and dismissed because of their "impersonal manufacture." [4] But the matter of by whom and how any work of art is created is tangential. The interest in this matter remains a tired and tiresome holdover from the centuries-long obsession with an aesthetic of virtuosity. In a democratic age attention must shift to the audience's reception of any work.

Traditionally, of course, all artistic styles may be said to be defined by repetitious elements such as their subject matter, tone, color, mood, materials, and so forth. Eighteenth century classicism, for example, is defined to a large extent by works that are distinct from those of other epochs but that also are repetitious when compared to one another. Virtuosity itself, moreover, invariably shifts toward repetition in any individual artist's body of work by defining the consistent vision and style for which a specific artist becomes well known and admired.

It is not simply, however, that television conforms to such generalized patterns of repetition as the other arts do. Rather, it is that repetition *defines* television aesthetically, structurally, and historically. Episodic sitcoms and dramas follow the same characters in the same settings as their situations vary slightly from week to week. Soap operas do the same, from day to day. NBC's *Tonight Show* provides a model for talk shows. The design of the set has become standardized and the show's structure is tightly patterned. The host's monologue is followed by several skits, at least one of which involves audience members. The main body of the show consists of a line up of guests who are never the same but who are predictably similar by type. The lead off guest, for example, is frequently an actor or an actress with a new feature film about to be released or who stars in a new TV show. Other celebrities are scheduled according to a standardized pecking order. Alongside the celebrities, common folk who have done something unusual or zany are slotted in, as are the guest singers and the stand-up comics.

National newscasts also follow a set pattern: the anchor's lead-in or hook; the story of the day, which may be international; the featured national political story normally focusing on the president and/or congressional leaders; human interest and follow up stories; an inevitable wrap up story that is a "softer" news piece and more upbeat in tone than the rest of the evening's coverage. Local news is even more rigid in its formula. Go anywhere in the country, from Portland, Maine, to Portland, Oregon, from Miami to Malibu, and turn on the local news at 10:00 or 11:00 p.m. Wherever you are, you can set your watch to the time that the weather will be reported or the day's sports will be summarized.

Does TV's reliance upon repetition hearken the emergence of a new human consciousness that is beckoning different people into an electronic global village in which they feel a genuine kinship to one another?[5] Does the fact that repetition defined ancient rites, rituals, myths, and legends mean that increasing numbers of us will connect with deeper yearnings of our minds and souls that are ancestral? Or does the idea of repetition, confronting us day in and day out on our TV sets, mark a further erosion of authentic community, hence condemning each of us to greater feelings of alienation? Does the idea of repetition compel us toward undiscriminating and mindless imitation of some centrally generated message? Or does TV beckon a wonderfully rich and full democratization of culture and society that is spreading to nearly every corner of the globe by leaps and bounds? All these questions are upon us. Today's arguments about television have sharpened our attention to any number of issues hotly debated since the late nineteenth century. What I see now, however, are increasing attempts to answer just such questions about modernization and change with reference to television itself. And I find these attempts to be highly speculative, imprecise, and misleading.

NOTES

1. I am indebted to the late Robert Plant Armstrong, my colleague in Aesthetic Studies at the University of Texas at Dallas, who exchanged with me so many ideas about aesthetics. His own three books on the subject are *Wellspring, The Powers of Presence*, and *The Affecting Presence*.

2. For a good description of this, see Parker Tyler, *Magic and Myth of the Movies* (New York: H. Holt & Co., 1947).

3. See, J. Dudley Andrew, *The Major Film Theories* (Oxford/New York: Oxford University Press, 1976). Still one of the best summaries of the thinking that formed the idea of the director as author, Andrew clarifies that this idea is not so much a theory as a "critical method." Critic Andrew Sarris most often is credited for introducing the *auteur* idea in the United States. For my views on the matter, see Paul Monaco, *Ribbons in Time: Movies and Society Since 1945* (Bloomington: Indiana University Press, 1987), pp. 34 ff.

4. For an excellent discussion of Macdonald's ideas in this context, see Hal Himmelstein, *On the Small Screen: New Approaches in Television and Video*

Criticism (New York: Praeger, 1981), pp. 4, 5.

    5. The term "global village" is attributed to Marshall McLuhan, *Understanding Media: The Extensions of Man* (New York: Signet Books, 1964).

3

Common Contemporary Themes

The way most Americans think and talk about TV is remarkable. Federal Communications Commission chairman Newton N. Minow's 1961 description of network television as "a vast wasteland" still is widely quoted. Hardly anyone is aware that at the end of that same year Minow was saying that when viewers on any given night could choose between a drama starring Julie Harris, a special with Yves Montand, or an exposé of a bookie joint, the networks already had led us out of the wasteland.[1] Following that logic, what should we make of television today when a substantial number of viewers can choose from scores of channels?

There is a lot of moaning about what's on TV. Complaints have been steady throughout television's half century of existence. From time to time their character and tone changes but the core idea remains unaltered. We are told that we are watching the wrong programs and too many of them. "Boob tube" and "couch potato" are common terms that nobody questions. Television, however, hardly has an exclusive hold on intellectual shallowness, dishonesty, and exaggeration in our culture.

Owners of $ 2,500 TV sets routinely call them idiot boxes, with little sense of self contradiction. Several years ago I knew a student who had a bumper sticker on his car that read: "Kill Your Television." On several occasions, however, I overheard him talking with other students about what he had seen the night before on *The David Letterman Show*. People consistently deny that they watch as much television as they actually do. The stigma attached to saying that you like television is strong. Recently, as a panelist on a televised discussion about violence and TV, the moderator asked me if people weren't watching TV "too much." His question implies that there is an answer. I don't believe that there is.

Ellen A. Wartella, the dean of the College of Communications at the University of Texas at Austin, maintains that "the United States is the only English-speaking nation in the world without media education in its public schools."[2] Whether this claim is literally true or not, American schools do spend billions of dollars trying to educate students to distinguish good writing from bad, but almost nothing on their understanding of the media arts. While the nation needs some substantive courses in television analysis and criticism, I would steer clear of the notion that the public schools need an elaborate curriculum or great expenditures of taxpayer dollars to explore television. What is needed, instead, is sound thinking about TV and where it fits into society and culture.

What is really wrong with television? Claims about the medium's negative impact upon society are rampant and come from various directions. Take, for example, the matter of how television covers the news. Andrew Tyndall, who tracks the time that television devotes to particular news stories found that from January through September 1995, the major American networks ABC, CBS, and NBC devoted twelve percent of their nightly newscasts to the O. J. Simpson murder trial. This was slightly more time than they devoted to the next two most covered stories *combined*: the war in Bosnia and the deadly bombing of the Murrah Federal Building in Oklahoma City.[3] A similar set of statistics reveals that the opening of the Berlin Wall in 1989 and its immediate aftermath warranted 252 minutes of network newscast coverage over a two-month period. The attack by people associated with Tonya Harding on rival Olympic figure skater Nancy Kerrigan garnered 263 minutes of coverage over a similar sixty days.[4]

In reading these statistics, I suspect that there is a widespread sense that we know what they mean. But what are the demonstrable social consequences of the amount of coverage devoted to specific stories or topics? The O. J. Simpson murder trial coincided with the period in which I did a substantial portion of the research for this book and began writing it. I followed a fair amount of the coverage of that trial, as well as commentary about it, on television. My interest in that trial, however, was in keeping with my own long term interests. I am a fan of Court TV. I saw considerable portions of the trial of William Kennedy Smith on rape charges. I watched some of the Menendez brothers' trial for the murder of their parents. Over the years, I have followed the trials of defendants both obscure and famous. I have even watched traffic court deliberations from various jurisdictions across the United States. I find legal argument and court procedures fascinating. Questions of guilt and innocence are intriguing to me, no matter what the charges against a defendant. Weighing the arguments and the evidence is part of seeing any trial, and awaiting a verdict can be exciting.

Interest in a particular trial may be stimulated by any number of factors, from the celebrity of defendants, such as O. J. Simpson or Joan Collins, to intimations of taboo subjects like incest and sexual abuse, as in the case of Lyle and Erik Menendez. If people wish to hear about the sensational, the macabre and the pathological, there is no clear judgment that we can make about this interest. In and of itself it is neither good nor bad. And it certainly is nothing new. Some critics are appalled by some of today's televison talk shows that feature such themes as "mothers who sleep with their daughters' boyfriends." But how does such behavior compare to killing your father and sleeping with your mother? While we venerate *Oedipus Rex* as a cornerstone of Western civilization, we condemn talk show hosts like Jenny Jones, Sally Jesse Raphael, Ricki Lake, and Jerry Springer.

We need not apologize for a culture that satisfies a wide range of interests. And we should never fall into the error of believing that widespread fascination with disturbing topics necessarily reveals something fundamentally flawed about our culture. The story of Faust, a man who sold his soul to the devil, inspired various highly regarded literary and dramatic works over several centuries. That we sometimes are fascinated by the darker side of the human spirit is only an acknowledgment that such a side surely exists and not necessarily an endorsement of it. *The Old Testament*, after all, contains tales of thievery and pillaging, lust and lechery, adultery and incest, rape and murder.

We may argue that the O. J. Simpson murder trial, or the William Kennedy Smith rape trial, have no practical connection to the lives of viewers and that their outcomes are of scant historical significance. But such a notion ignores the fact that individuals relate to events for different and complex reasons. If most citizens devoted interest to news and public affairs in direct proportion to their own narrow and immediate interests, most would pay greatest attention to any and all pending revisions in the U.S. tax code. Beyond that, they might focus on issues of broad economic importance, such as the negotiation of an international tariff and trade agreement. And the fascination with O. J. Simpson's trial for murder was limited neither to audiences in the United States nor to the least well-educated sectors of the population. Six months after Simpson was acquitted of criminal charges he was the invited guest of the one-hundred-and-seventy-five-year-old Debating Society at Oxford University. From its founding, the American Republic has made court proceedings open to the public and from time to time, dating all the way back to the late eighteenth century, sensational cases have drawn the kind of public attention and media notoriety that turned them into legends.

Tonya Harding and Nancy Kerrigan hardly interested me at all. The competition between these two ladies of the rink never caught my imagination. I couldn't buy this story as an engaging combat between the ice princess from New England and the upstart little roughneck from the pine woods of Oregon. But other people in the potential viewing audience were interested. The TV networks determined this, and hence provided for on going coverage of the physical assault on Kerrigan and its aftermath. In this instance, to what kind of taste were the TV broadcasters appealing? Was the audience full of devotees of the nuances and intricacies of figure skating as sport? Were people tuned in to delight in seeing the long-standing athletic competition between two young ladies turn nasty and ugly? Could viewer interest really have been with Tonya's oafish husband and his band of mean-spirited pranksters who whacked Nancy on the knee?

News is storytelling, and TV news is story-telling with sharp and terse commentary, bountiful pictures, and a compelling sense of immediacy. News is about unusual or significant behavior and events. The unusual and the significant includes the exceptional and the inspiring. It also includes the bizarre and the degrading. What would any of us really make out of an eleven o'clock newscast reporting that during the day 21,318 commercial airline flights had taken off and landed safely in the United States? That we want to know about the one flight that crashed betrays nothing necessarily morbid or insensitive about us. Nor does the interest that humans have in fiction and drama about flawed characters, crimes of passion, criminal escapades, unrequited love, or death and dying mean that our human sensibilities are warped or perverse.

Lots of hype surrounds TV events and shows. But the impulse toward such hype is not television's folly. It is inherent in human beings.

Without it we would not strive toward ideas and values that are abstract. With it we have to be continuously assessing and judging what we see and hear. The real issue confronting us with regard to television is how to encourage sharp reasoning and clear thinking about all that it presents to us. The false issue is blaming television for our social ills, as if changing what is on television would make those problems go away.

In one postmortem on the O. J. Simpson criminal trial David Gelernter of Yale University posed a fundamental question about journalistic judgment, citing a headline from one of the nation's most prestigious newspapers: "'Racism of a Rogue Officer,' *The New York Times* announced in print, 'Casts Suspicions on Police Nationwide.' How much consideration did it give to the headline 'Murder of Mrs. Simpson Casts Suspicion on Black Males Nationwide'?"[5] The impulse to make much out of little and to generalize is not only basic to television, but also to human thought. We have to constantly sift through information and opinion, deciding what is important and what is not. And, after all, there is little evidence that TV news holds extraordinary sway over viewers. Studies discover that viewers are highly skeptical about believing what they see and hear on television about public affairs. TV news not only is *not* hypnotic, it is apparently not even very convincing. [6] Responding to a questionnaire, fully two-thirds of the American viewing public faults news reporting in the United States for being intentionally biased and manipulative.[7]

Even more disconcerting is the common idea that fictions on television account for poor choices and criminal behavior in society. In 1992, the Vice President of the United States, Dan Quayle, drew global attention when he criticized an episode from the popular TV series *Murphy Brown*. In it the main character, a professional in her forties, decides to give birth to a baby without marrying the child's father. Quayle claimed that this fictional portrayal was providing a negative example for unwed teenage mothers whose situation fuels considerable social and economic misery in the United States.[8] But what is the evidence that a 15-year-old living in the inner city actually guides her decisions by taking a fictional forty-year-old journalist as her role model? The public is highly inclined to believe that such a 15-year-old is likely to get an undesirable message from the show, namely, that it is just fine to become an unwed mother. Why doesn't the public believe, alternatively, that she might get a *positive* message from the show? That it is desirable to have the freedom and security of a well-educated person who has achieved a responsible and well-paying job is just as much what the character Murphy Brown is about!

Across the political divide from Mr. Quayle, eighteen months later, the Attorney General, Janet Reno, threatened TV-broadcasters with censorship (*legislation* is the polite term) if they did not cut back on the fictional violence reaching America's television screens. Ms. Reno attributed the ultimate evil on the little screen to the asocial antics of two crudely drawn animated characters featured in their own show called *Beavis and Butt-head*.[9] Hence, the American public is left to believe that the nation's highest law enforcement official is convinced that she has discovered a direct connection between the naughty antics of this cartoon duo and violence on America's streets: gang wars, drive-by shootings, pathological serial killing, car-jackings, breaking and entering, murder, mugging, and mayhem!

Rampant this kind of speculation certainly is; well-documented it surely is not. This entire line of thinking is grotesquely convoluted and baffling, and yet it appears to be widely accepted. Talking about the campaigners who consistently attribute negative social effects to television, the British scholar Martin Barker writes: "Their claim is that the materials they judge to be 'harmful' can only influence us by trying to make us the same as them. So horrible things will make us horrible–not horrified. Terrifying things will make us terrifying–not terrified." [10] The single-mindedness of such claims should serve as a first warning to us of their shallowness.

Moreover, counter evidence nearly always is omitted from discussion over the possible influences of the media. As a child in the late 1940s, I was an avid fan of movie cartoons. Like many children, I was amused and delighted by the typical antics that presented scenes like beleaguered mice attaching explosives to the rear end of a sassy pussy cat and blasting him into the nether reaches of space. Yet, it never occurred to me to copy such behavior in real life. And although I was a devoted fan of Bugs Bunny, I never was tempted to ask my parents to buy me his favorite food--carrots.

From the 1930s to the mid-1960s, the Motion Picture Association of America ("Hollywood") made movies under the "Hays Code" which placed rigid limitations on fictional representations of crime and sex. Kisses on screen were limited to a couple of seconds and never with the mouths open. Scenes of a bedroom, even that of a married couple, showed two beds, lest the sight of one bed for two arouse the prurient interest and erotic passions of the average moviegoer. Criminals might be depicted, but only if their capture and punishment were assured by the movie's end.

From its inception television in America was even more rigidly controlled, given the self-censorship of the networks, the cautious attitudes of advertisers, and governmental regulation by the Federal Communications Commission (FCC). Network executives at CBS, for example, even made sure that the cameras never tilted down to show Elvis Presley's gyrating hips during his TV-premiere on *The Ed Sullivan Show* in 1956. America's children and teenagers were kept safe from even a glimpse of the King's bump-and-grind.

Well into the 1960s, both movies and television in the United States unabashedly portrayed conventional and puritanical values. Nonetheless, the audience nurtured as children on just these media grew into the young adults who gave the nation its sexual revolution and a full-fledged drug culture. In all the talk and writing about media effects, especially about the potential dangers of film and television fare, this history is commonly overlooked. When we are considering why we believe that violence and sex in movies and TV frequently find their way into lived behavior, we need to be asking why wholesome and inoffensive movies and television programming did not prevent the counterculture changes that occurred in society during the late 1960s?

The other counter evidence that is almost always ignored on the question of media influence and effects comes from other countries. In a rare commentary about what is on television elsewhere, a writer for *Time Magazine* concluded: "Channel surf elsewhere and U.S. television begins to seem as though it were run by so many Roman Catholic schoolgirls. . . . In Japan . . . prime-time TV is a mixed menu of soft-core porn, bloodletting drama, and violent animation."[11] Much the same is true, by the way, in many European countries and has been for a number of years. Yet, the rates for homicide and other violent crime in all these countries vary considerably from the United States, as do the statistics for illegitimate births and school performance as measured by standardized tests. Viewed comparatively, the claims of causal connections between what is on television and what is going on in America's schools, its bedrooms, and its streets is nonsensical.

Underlying such nonsense is a widely held belief that fictional movies and television programs represent equivalencies to real life. There is continuing anger about how certain characters are portrayed in films and/or TV programs and public arguments about such portrayals. Some claim that *The Godfather* films as well as other fictional media productions about the Mafia are denigrating to Italian Americans. There are complaints when African Americans are portrayed as street people or muggers. The image of women in the media has drawn extraordinary attention since the end of the 1960s. Indeed, this entire topic of media representation draws a double whammy that fuels all sorts of agendas. Feminists can find in a predictable "buddy" film like *Thelma and Louise* a parable of emancipation in the antics of a pair of women on the run. Conservatives complain that marriage and the family are treated with savage contempt in the movies and on TV. Liberals argue that being unmarried or homosexual assures negative representation in the media. Lawyers do not like their media image. Friends of the unfortunate are offended by scenes in movies or on TV in which the homeless appear menacing or threatening. Friends of the animals condemn scenes set at a rodeo or on a hunting trip. Many African Americans object when Blacks are portrayed as criminal characters, but also complain about representations of high-achieving Black families, as seen on TV's *Cosby Show* or *The Jeffersons*, which they consider to be misleading and unrealistic. Social theorist Paul Ehrlich once proposed that a new federal agency be set up to effectively limit population growth in the United States. Ehrlich wanted the agency to promote what he called "voluntary birth control programs." He also argued that it should have the power to prohibit the broadcast of *all* shows on television "featuring large families."[12]

At base, such thinking and arguing has less to do with these media than with the presumed audience for them, which is believed to be undiscriminating and stupid. This assumption holds that much of the audience will be unduly and negatively influenced by what it sees and hears. But what is the proof for this claim? Audiences for films and TV behave with a great deal of particular discrimination toward productions and their stars. Amid a smorgasbord of media offerings that look like they have much in common with one another, individual taste functions as being extraordinarily precise. Some of us like this thriller but not that one; Glenn Close but not Meryl Streep; *Baywatch* but not *Melrose Place*; *The X-Files* but not *Startrek: Voyager*; Jay Leno but not David Letterman. Movie and television culture is unique at specific levels of discrimination and taste. Responses to both these media are extraordinarily precise at this level. Most popular and serious commentary on film and television ignores this. The precision of viewer attitudes is part of the complexity of these media and their appeal.

Contemporary society is awash in wild, but widely believed, claims about the movies, television, and the audiences for them. This, combined with perceptions of the sophisticated electronic technology of movies, video, and TV, contributes to the widespread fear of the manipulative powers of these media. Aside from the rhetoric that maintains their acute manipulative powers over audiences, little evidence supports these fears. Such claims really will not stand up to an examination of them. Moreover, in order to stand up they must be premised on a view that takes humans to be, in great numbers, lacking in rationality and discrimination. Given the insufficient evidence to demonstrate the claimed effects of film and television, as well as the fact that humans are neither as mindless nor as uncritical as they would have to be for such effects to influence them as is claimed, this entire line of thinking is on very shaky ground indeed.

NOTES

1. *Variety*, December 13, 1961.

2. Ellen A. Wartella, "The Context of Television Violence," The Carroll C. Arnold Distinguished Lecture, Needham Heights, MA, Allyn and Bacon, 1997.

3. Michael Gartner, "O.J. Circus, Blame TV," *USA Today*, October 3, 1995, p. 11A.

4. Cited in an editorial, *The Bozeman Daily Chronicle*, July 15, 1994, p. 4.

5. David Gelernter, "The Real Story of Orenthal James," *National Review*, October 9, 1995, p. 47.

6. *USA Today*, May 13, 1996.

7. Judith Valente, "Do You Believe What Newspeople Tell You?" *Parade Magazine*, March 2, 1997.

8. See, Richard Zoglin, "Sitcom Politics," *Time*, September 21, 1992, pp. 44-47; Fred Barnes, "Insurrection," *The New Republic*, June 22, 1992, pp. 12, 13; Andrew Rosenthal, "Quayle's Moment," *New York Times Magazine*, July 3, 1992, pp. 10-13. Initially, most commentary criticized Quayle, but for a different opinion, see James Bowman, "Too Much Mr. Nice Guy," *National Review*, June 22, 1992, pp. 21, 22.

9. See, *U.S. News and World Report*, November 1, 1993, p. 11. Taking up Reno's side, see Gerald Howard, "Divide and Deride: Prevalence of Stupidity in the Mass Media," *The Nation*, December 20, 1993, pp. 772, 773. For more critical views of Reno's position, see Frank McConnell, "Art Is Dangerous:

Beavis & Butt-head, for Example," *Commonweal*, January 14, 1994, pp. 28-30; Jon Katz, "Beavis and Butt-head," *Rolling Stone*, March 24, 1995, p. 45, amusingly points out that United States Senator Ernest Hollings (Democrat, South Carolina) took up Reno's criticism, repeatedly calling the show "Buff-Coat and Beaver" on the Senate floor. The criticism spread wide. See, for example, Miriam Horn, "Teaching Television Violence," *U.S. News and World Report*, December 27, 1993, p. 91 which recounts CNN-founder and media mogul Ted Turner's testimony to Congress that TV is "the single most significant factor causing violence in America."

10. Martin Barker, "The Newson Report: A Case Study in 'Common Sense,'" in *Ill Effects: The Media/Violence Debate*, edited by Martin Barker and Julian Petley (London/New York: Routledge, 1997), p. 23.

11. Ginia Bellafante, "So What's On in Tokyo?" *Time*, February 16, 1996.

12. Alexander Volkoh, "How Green Is Our Valley?," *Reason*, March, 1995, p. 62.

4

Agendas, Politics, and Television

In 1992, I was teaching as a Fulbright Guest Professor at the University of Essen in Germany. One morning local newspapers carried a story from the United States that bewildered my students. It caused me to embark upon an examination of one of the more vexing issues in contemporary media criticism. The story was about the vice president of the United States, Dan Quayle. While visiting a spelling bee he had urged a youthful contestant to add an *e* incorrectly to his spelling of the word potato.[1]

What crossed my mind first was how and why this event had come to be considered newsworthy. How odd it would have been to have awakened, back home in the United States, to a front-page news story about Chancellor Helmut Kohl of Germany misspelling "Kartoffel." As I reflected on this news story I had difficulty imagining a similar incident involving any other politician, no matter what his or her nationality or party affiliation, receiving the same attention. The incident occurred on the eve of a campaign for the presidency, but it struck me that even had Quayle's running mate, President George Bush, made the same gaffe it was unlikely that it would have drawn similar media attention. What was involved was something unique and peculiar to the public *persona* of Dan Quayle. The reason a spelling error by Quayle was news had to do both with specifics about him and how news, in general, is made.

From that moment in the summer of 1988 when then presidential candidate Bush selected Quayle, a little-known junior senator from Indiana, as his running mate the press had made much of the latter's presumed intellectual limitations. True, Quayle's initial appearances before the media were awkward. The youthful candidate, who has exceptionally pale-colored eyes, struck some commentators as having the look of a scared and startled rabbit. Quayle's entry onto the national scene was less than scintillating, but there was little about it to warrant the media assault that ensued. Immediately, the press began to imply that his unease must be the result of a flawed intellect. Following quickly on the heels of suggestions of his intellectual shallowness came journalistic inquiry into the candidate's undergraduate academic record and his grade point average on college courses. This, in itself, was highly unusual. American culture shows noticeably little interest in the academic records of individuals in most walks of life, inclining toward far more pragmatic assessments of subsequent accomplishments.

What is most interesting to me about the Quayle spelling bee story is how it illustrates one of the most well-demonstrated points of contemporary media theory, namely, *agenda setting*.[2] Dan Quayle's misspelling of *potato* could not have been rendered noteworthy, let alone newsworthy, were it not for the media's long-standing questioning and criticizing of his intelligence. Without this context the story was nil! And this context had been created through four years of media focus. A story on Quayle's spelling error registered with a sizable portion of the public as news because so many people could connect promptly with its presumed meaning and significance.

The Quayle spelling bee story may first raise questions about the intentions of the reporters. For some the incident will be understood as a matter of media bias pure and simple. Although I am not eager to make excuses on behalf of reporters, it is wise to suspend judgment on this matter, in order to delve deeper into what it can reveal. To recapitulate quickly, in his initial appearances Quayle left poor impressions. He seemed unusually ill at ease before the cameras and microphones for someone on a campaign that might put him but a heartbeat away from the presidency. The press corps that followed him on the campaign trail observed and reported his slips of the tongue and mangled syntax. In and of themselves, mixed metaphors and malapropisms may not be all that rare among public figures whose every word in public is recorded. But Quayle's slips did appear to be more numerous than many other politicians'. Moreover, and most importantly, the 1988 election campaign proved to be relatively uninteresting. The fortunes of the Democratic ticket of Michael Dukakis and Lloyd Bentsen peaked early, and its chances waned quickly.   What reporters found disconcerting about Quayle developed into an image of him that provided a good story. The perpetuation of that image depended upon the consistency of its repetition across the media.   But the impact of that repetition, and the strength eventually accorded to it, depended finally upon the response to it by a substantial portion of the public.

What the best mass communication research concludes is that the news industry doesn't tell its readers and viewers *what to think* so much as it points them toward *what to think about*. This one generalization has been well sustained through three decades of inquiry and analysis, both empirical and speculative. But while this notion of the agenda-setting capacity of the media is well established, it is far less clear as to just how influential agenda setting really is.

In this context, I am reminded of an incident related to me by a producer/writer friend who visited Prague not long before the collapse of communism in Eastern Europe. Waiting to meet someone with whom he was to discuss a film project, he found himself in a hotel lobby where what he recognized as a radio transmission was blaring in Czech. Frustrated by the lateness of the other person, the loudness of the radio, and the fact that he understood no Czech, he walked over to the radio and attempted to change the station—which could not be done! Nor could he change the volume! Both he discovered were set and could not be regulated by anyone, either hotel guest or staff, as was verified to him when the desk clerk returned from his break. This mandatory delivery system, in the peculiar mode of Eastern European communism, was monolithic and unfree. But this patently is not true of the delivery of cultural products elsewhere, nor is it true of such delivery in the Czech Republic since the fall of communism. Radio or television knobs can be tightened down and made immovable, but no one should overlook the real lesson to be drawn from the unrelenting control of the press, the media, and every other aspect of art and culture in Eastern Europe under communism. When these regimes fell, one after another, at the end of the 1980s, the propaganda apparatus in all of them had provided no assurance at all for belief in its messages. People simply had not bought the ideas that the state's media had been feeding to them.

For a number of years, it has been claimed that news, public affairs programming, and documentaries seen on television in the United States carry liberal biases. Public interest programming and social documentary often are perceived to commonly treat problems from the perspective of the Left. Critics argue that this fact determines the content and the tone of the political coverage on national television in the United States. Political reporting, hence, is frequently claimed to be one-sided, favoring the Democratic Party and policy positions associated with it.[3] Much of this suspicion comes from the political Right, of course, but even *Time Magazine* in 1995 acknowledged its astonishment at the pronounced liberal biases it discovered among national journalists, as based upon the magazine's survey of them.[4]

Cultures do have establishments, of course, and in contemporary democracies these are defined not by ties of kinship, but rather by the sharing of ideas and attitudes that have gained currency. In itself, this is not necessarily bad, but it does mean that certain forms of establishment thinking come to easily dominate specific professions such as journalism. Such thinking, moreover, is further exaggerated in news reporting because journalists commonly seek out commentary by relying heavily upon established academics and official government sources. Such experts often hold the positions that they do precisely because their thinking reflects a strong degree of agreement with what is commonly held to be conventional wisdom. Also, national news agencies and broadcasters are concentrated in New York City, Washington, D.C., and Atlanta. They surely value objectivity, but they simultaneously reflect a high degree of cohesiveness based upon the shared views found within the comparatively narrow social and intellectual circumstances in which they live and socialize.

On the other hand, accusations are equally strong from the Left that "the news media distort the image that most middle-class Americans have of racial and ethnic minorities. A good deal of the media's racial and ethnic stereotyping can be attributed to the fact that crime stories constitute much of standard news coverage."[5] In fact, to appreciate that this contention may be as valid as the one that holds that the national news has a liberal bias, it is necessary to emphasize the geographic distinction in coverage. *Local* television news throughout the United States heavily emphasizes the reporting of violent crime. Especially in urban areas, a good deal of such reporting does focus upon neighbor-hoods and populations in which crime rates are high. Surely, this emphasis alone contributes to an image of the areas and their populations that are reported upon that may be interpreted as constituting a negative agenda.

It is one thing to generalize about typical types of coverage and to point out that news stories inevitably follow leads that run along the tracks laid down by larger agendas. It is a far more open and vexing question to try to determine to what degree the images created by such coverage and agendas are distorted or not. And beyond the issue of that distortion is the even larger one of how any individual viewer may interpret and respond to any given information.

There is no predetermined path from any particular bit of data to any specific conclusion about it. We are all constantly filtering out biases and making judgments based on assessments from our individual points of view. When I first learned of Dan Quayle's gaffe at the spelling bee, I was immediately sympathetic to him. Conventional logic might say that I should have been appalled like many other Americans apparently were, concluding, "Aha, what a bozo." Instead, since I have a lot of trouble remembering correct spellings myself, I empathized with Quayle. After all, I am forever consulting dictionaries and spell checks on computers. And having written and published several books, I thank the heavens for copy editors and proofreaders who can still catch all the misspellings that I have inevitably overlooked.

We all respond to information, process it, and reach conclusions about it based upon many variables of reception. Since 1991 the national media has been reporting challenges to President Bill Clinton's honesty and integrity, ranging from accusations of womanizing to his involvement in the land deals and the tangled finances of an affair called "Whitewater," as well as his lying about how he obtained a draft deferment during the Viet Nam War. However, these accusations and exposés have not translated necessarily into political negatives for Clinton. To alter a cliché that originated in the Viet Nam era: "What if they set an agenda and no one came?"

Some people are concerned about the issues of character surrounding Clinton, and surely the names of Gennifer Flowers, Paula Jones, James and Susan McDougal, Webster Hubble, and Monica Lewinsky are well enough known nationally. It is not so much a case of inattention to these matters by the news media, however, as it is the lack of response by substantial numbers of Americans to the issues that they raise. We may take interest in a story, but that does not determine anything about our interpretation of its meaning and value. Just about everybody in the United State knows that Quayle misspelled *potato*. For some people, that means that he's a dummy. For others, that means that he makes a lot of gaffes in public. For others, that means absolutely nothing at all.

Apparently, many Americans believe that Bill Clinton has had sexual relations outside his marriage. To some that means that he has an active libido, referred to jokingly as a "zipper problem." Others who believe the same accusations call him a skirt chaser, with a mild tone of condemnation, while for still others he is nothing less than a sexual predator. For some, the issue is his sexual behavior, of which they disapprove. For others, sexuality between consenting adults is a private matter and they are interested only in whether Clinton has lied about such incidents or urged others to do so. Sill others consider lying about private matters an understandable peccadillo and not an indication of any real moral flaw. As a Democratic party pollster, Geoff Garin, notes: "It's not that people don't pay attention to these things. People pay attention and are willing to hold their judgment. . . ."[6] When accusations are called into question, the public does display widespread reasonable doubt. And even when voters find evidence sufficient for them to doubt the quality of a man's character or his ability to spell correctly, they apparently still may be willing to vote for him. The range of responses to such incidents and revelations has little to do with whether they are reported adequately, but rather with the standards by which individuals choose to interpret the meaning of them.

We may agree or disagree with someone's reasoning on these matters as we each come to an assessment of the credibility and centrality of these matters as they pertain to either Dan Quayle or Bill Clinton. What must be emphasized is that different people reach different conclusions–which often conflict with one another–on the basis of exactly the same information that is reported by the media. Whether you believe that bad spelling, or adulterous affairs, or prevaricating are grounds to disqualify someone from public office has nothing to do with TV.

Television news and informational programming may set agendas, but individuals interpret each and every piece of news in light their own *personal* agenda. A longitudinal study funded by the Pew Foundation, the results of which were published early in 1997, indicated that since the 1950s Americans have become progressively skeptical about believing the news and informational programming that they see on television. Interestingly, the respondents surveyed in this study distrust national news coverage far more than they distrust local news on television.[7]

Still, a counter argument holds that there is evidence of the population responding immediately and strongly to the reporting of certain events on television, which, therefore, must demonstrate the enormously manipulative power of television. This argument, however, must be analyzed carefully. For example, immediately after Earvin "Magic" Johnson announced his retirement from the National Basketball Association in November 1991 because he had tested positive for the HIV virus, AIDS hotlines and information centers across the country were flooded with phone calls and inquiries on HIV testing. Yet, what I find most interesting about this incident is the fact that the increase in the number of such calls, while immediate and dramatic, was also remarkably short-lived. In less than a week's time the volume of calls returned to the level at which it had been before Johnson's announcement. And, furthermore, in spite of the substantially increased number of callers right after Johnson's announcement, the percentage of them who tested positive for the virus was at precisely the same rate as it had been among callers who had been phoning before Johnson went on TV.[8]

A great deal of caution is warranted when it comes to assumptions about news, informational programming, and television effects. While the media surely set agendas and while immediate short-term reactions to stories on TV may be strong, the filters through which viewers perceive and react to news and information on television are complex.

I vividly recall teaching a class several days after television cameras had followed O. J. Simpson's notorious freeway drive in the white Bronco as he was fleeing from the law. There was not one student among the forty or so in that class who was not convinced that media coverage already had so biased the case against Simpson that he would never be able to get a fair trial. They were united in believing that Simpson already had been convicted by TV because of this coverage. Specific claims like this come and go, right alongside the general suspicions about television's shortcomings and its negative impact on society and culture. Indeed, it is often difficult to conclude anything from both serious and popular commentary about television except that many people believe that the medium constitutes some horrible intrusion upon the otherwise systematic and normative development of civilization itself.

Just about anything associated with television is grist for the mills of the cultural critics and the academic pundits. Take, for example, the concern that television favors sound bites, which are thought to undermine our communal and civic well-being by trivializing political discourse. Since TV appears to favor the repetition of short statements that appeal to the ear and are easily held in memory the claim is advanced that this must be compromising depth and insight in our public life. This is, however, a shallow assessment and critique; after all, a sound bite is simply a terse and pithy articulation of a complicated or seminal notion. Throughout history just such phrases have expressed important ideas:

> "I think, therefore I am."
> "We hold these truths to be self-evident, that all men are created equal."
> "Give me liberty, or give me death."
> "This is the Age of Reason."
> "Existence precedes essence."
> "Workers of the world unite, you have nothing to lose but your chains."
> "First comes eating; then comes morality."
> "All the world is a stage."

Profound or provocative ideas and insights may be articulated succinctly. All of us use such phrases, but only some such articulations become known to posterity. Queen Marie Antoinette's, "Let them eat cake," reflects well enough the Old Regime's arrogant insensitivity toward widespread poverty and misery in France during the early stages of the 1789 Revolution. Two hundred years from now it is unlikely that anyone will be citing George Bush's 1988 campaign pledge: "Read my lips, no new taxes." In the short run, however, just those six words haunted him in his reelection attempt in 1992. After Bush's 1990 compromise with Congress to raise taxes, his earlier campaign promise came to stand as a betrayal of principle to those who desired no new taxes or pointed to a presumed flaw in is his character even among those who did.

There is widespread fear that television either is, or soon will be, devastating to healthy political discourse around the globe. Many people believe that TV's repetitious patterning, combined with its penchant for glorifying simple messages that are cleverly phrased, will bring on societal catastrophe. Yet the great political and societal catastrophes of the twentieth century, Nazism and Communism, both predated television. And the latter deteriorated and collapsed in chronological step with the international rise of television.

Nonetheless, images of a mindless society and a wasteland culture based upon the triumph of technological control over individuals, as popularized in George Orwell's novel entitled *1984*, remain popular. They do so in spite of the fact that Orwell's novel, although great fiction, scores absolute zero as prophecy. Chronologically the actual year 1984 stands in the middle of a two-decade period marked by the unprecedented collapse of authoritarian states and totalitarian regimes all across the political spectrum. The rise of democracy occurred on every continent and among all kinds of people, some of whom were considered good bets for such change and others who were not. From the end of the fascistic regimes of Franco and Salazar on the Iberian Peninsula in the mid 1970s, through the fall of Soviet Communism across Eastern Europe and in Russia itself, and from the emergence of peaceful elections in Central and Latin America to constitutional reform in South Africa, democratization has swept the globe.[9]

Alongside the global rise of television since the mid-1970s there has occurred a parallel end to authoritarian and repressive regimes that is unique in history. Whether these two phenomena are linked causally is not the question here. It must be emphasized, however, that the global spread of television has nowhere meant the triumph of repressive governments. The boob tube, whatever else its failings, has not fostered the triumph of Big Brother. Keep in mind just *when* the Nazis and Communists flourished. Better the idiot box, whatever some may consider to be its shortcomings, than the idiot brigades!

NOTES

1. See, Paul Slansky and Steve Radlauer, "Airhead Apparent," *Esquire*, August, 1992, pp. 117-121. Sidney Blumenthal, "Dan's Big Plans," *Vanity Fair*, September, 1992, pp. 210-216 argues that various gaffes by Quayle really have hurt him politically. See also, Michael Lewis, "The Boy in the Bubble," *The New Republic*, October 19, 1992, p. 25 for yet another read on the situation.

2. In professional circles the term was established by the mid-1970s. See, Maxwell E. McCombs and D. L. Shaw, "The Agenda-Setting Function of the Mass Media," *Public Opinion Quarterly*, 36, 1976, pp. 176-187.

3. There is a substantial volume of commentary on the liberal bias of the American media. A classic book on the topic is William A. Rusher's, *The Coming Battle for the Media: Curbing the Power of the Media Elite* (New York: Morrow, 1988). From an opposite perspective, see Christopher Hanson, "Media Bashing," *Columbia Journalism Review*, November/December, 1992. Hanson acknowledges the liberal credentials of a majority of journalists and agrees, for example, that coverage of the 1992 Republican National Convention in Houston leaned toward the Democrats. He finds, however, that this was balanced by intensive "media scrutiny" of the Clinton presidential campaign.

4. *Time*, June 5, 1995, p. 16.

5. Patricia Hynds, "Balancing Bias in the News: Critical Questions Can Help Viewers, *Media and Values*, Fall, 1992.

6. *The Washington Post National Weekly Edition*, January 26, 1998.

7. Reported on *The Newshour With Jim Lehrer*, PBS, April 7, 1997

8. Everett M. Rogers, "When the Media Have Strong Effects: Intermedia Processes," Paper delivered at the SCA National Conference, November 14, 1996, San Diego, CA.

9. See Francis Fukuyama, *The End of History and the Last Man* (New York: Avon Books, 1992).

5

Globalization and Television

The term *global village* trips lightly from the lips of people in every generation everywhere in the world. The abundant evidence that supports such a concept appears to be incontrovertible. Since World War II the evolution in transportation has been extensive. If you have the money to do so, today you can fly from Paris to New York on the Concorde and arrive at a time earlier than when you departed. The revolution in communications is just as startling. By e-mail I can get a message to a friend in Berlin as fast and reliably as I can get a message to a colleague down the hall in the same building on the university campus where I teach. What happens in Peking or Paraguay gets reported to us as quickly as what happens in Philadelphia or Peoria. What Hollywood produces for movie theaters and for television plays to equally enthusiastic audiences in Bozeman, Montana, Berlin, Germany, and Bogota, Colombia. While vacationing in the interior of the island of Sicily a few years ago, I saw a man dressed in traditional black peasant clothes riding a donkey. As he approached, I saw how old and weathered he looked. I also saw that he was wearing a black baseball cap with a Los Angeles Raiders emblem.

But how and why the world has become smaller and, more importantly, what this may mean, is a complex matter. It is easy to overlook how extensively the development of civilization always has depended upon the flow of ideas and images between peoples. That movement has certainly accelerated at the end of the twentieth century, but influences crossing the continents and the boundaries between nations long have been at the heart of the collective human experience. For example, pasta dishes are now included on the menus of restaurants all across the United States. Pasta made its way to the United States from Italy, but it had gotten there after Marco Polo discovered it in China in the thirteenth century. Roman Catholic parishioners in Bozeman, Montana, Berlin, Germany, and Bogota, Colombia all were still celebrating Mass in the same universal Latin language into the mid 1960s. Ideas, images, languages, styles of dress, and cuisine never have really known strict geographic or political boundaries, and in many instances have been transmitted against great odds or outright prohibition. Since the beginning of recorded history there have never been pure cultures just as there have never been pure ethnic groups or races.

Nonetheless, great numbers of people, both abroad and in the United States, believe that they can understand the spread of popular culture worldwide in the late twentieth century. To them "American cultural imperialism" provides a simplistic but satisfying way to account for why the taste for so much music, film, and television is so similar in so many places. For many people, this explanation also provides the grounds for characterizing the United States as both the bully of the global village and its idiot as well.

Several years ago I was invited to speak at the Institute for Advanced Studies in Commerce in Dunkerque, France. My announced topic was "Hollywood in The World," which I presented as a historic overview of how the American film industry had come to dominate global commerce in theatrical films so completely. Taking an open approach to my task, I soon found myself debating with a student in the audience. Our point of departure was her version of the contempt, that was widespread and widely publicized in France at the time, toward the Euro-Disney theme park that was just then opening outside Paris.[1] My antagonist maintained that this entertainment center, modeled on the highly successful Disney parks in Anaheim, California and Orlando, Florida, was one more dreadful example of American cultural imperialism encroaching upon Europe.

The entire Disneyland concept itself is an ambitious spin-off from Disney's animated movies, taking a range of cartoon characters and their familiar stories to form the core of a family amusement center. When I pressed my young adversary, however, to explain just what was the danger that she perceived from Euro-Disney, she summarized it as "your (the United States') attempt to impose upon me (and other Europeans) your vision of the world." Well now, I found this to be a real mouthful. Here was an energetic defender of French culture and civilization, who could invoke the philosophic importance of figures from Descartes to Sartre, powerhouses of the Age of Reason, like Montesquieu or Diderot, literary figures from Abélard to Zola, and innovators in the social sciences such as Émile Durkheim or Jacques Lacan, terrified by a vision of the world advanced by a talking mouse!

It turned out that she was fearful of becoming "Americanized." By comparison, I asked her: "If you bought and drove a Mercedes would you be afraid of becoming "Germanized?" Or, if I buy and drink a bottle of Dom Perignon champagne are my body, mind, soul, and spirit flirting with becoming French? Pizza has surpassed hamburgers as the most popular food in the United States. Latté, capuccino, and espresso have spread their caffeine-laced tentacles across America and can now be found in tantalizingly obscure locales. Are many Americans thus fearful of becoming "Italianized," whatever that might mean?

In democracies, control over all such cultural inroads and innovations finally resides with individuals. Indeed, this function of personal choice is clear enough in the example of Euro-Disney itself. Since it opened in 1992 this theme park has hardly proven to be an economic boon for its operators. Over its first several years attendance was poor to modest and has continued to run behind hopes.[2] The European public has not been seduced by this attraction, although interpreting this failure correctly is not a simple matter. It does not mean that there is a general decline in the popularity of this kind of mass culture abroad. Europeans are seeing more Hollywood movies and TV than ever before. Big Macs sell briskly from Piccadilly Circus to the Kremlin. Coke and Pepsi flow from Dublin to Vladivostok. Even the Disney cartoon characters, which are used in all kinds of entertainment and merchandising, show no decline in popularity. The specific business problems of the Euro-Disney theme park account for its poor performance. Many Europeans vacation differently than Americans, especially families. The climate in the north of France really is *much* less amenable than in Anaheim, California or Orlando, Florida for tramping around a theme park. The cost of admission, food, lodging, and the attractions at Euro-Disney are evidently out of line with the disposable income available to much of the target audience in Europe.

Euro-Disney has suffered from these specific miscalculations. Its financial troubles, however, inevitably will be interpreted in broader contexts. The tendency toward such interpretation is fueled by simplistic assumptions about the Americanization of global culture as well as being rooted in cultural resentments that are based upon a concept of the national identity of culture. Surely there are cultural differences that can be ascribed to groups, but their variety does not adhere to the limits of national boundaries. Tastes today are likely more predictable by generation, or age cohort, than by looking at what passport someone holds. The complexity of how art and culture have changed globally during the twentieth century is at the heart of the matter.

At the end of the First World War, Hollywood became the preeminent, global center of a movie industry that was popular with people everywhere. Ever since then Hollywood has dominated the motion pictures and, subsequently, video and television as much as Florence dominated painting during the Renaissance or Stratford-upon-Avon dominated Elizabethan drama. The term Hollywood, moreover, has come to stand for a variety of tastes, diversions, and lifestyles. Hollywood commonly may mean glittery but shallow, vulgar, and undifferentiated. At the same time, the term also suggests technical accomplishment and polish, spectacular effects, and a mastery over a kind of storytelling that is highly effective.

Hollywood was invented by Eastern European immigrants to the United States. A majority of them were Jewish, and at the time of the First World War they moved their businesses from New York and New Jersey to Southern California far removed from the established centers of American cultural, political, and economic power on the east coast.[3] To some observers, the goal of those who established Hollywood was to find cheap real estate in a setting affording all sorts of terrain, including mountains, seashore, dessert, and plains, as well as a moderate year-round climate for outdoor filming. Others, however, interpreted the move as reflecting a rejection of what was then the patrician and traditional Anglo-Saxon and Protestant culture of America's eastern cities.

Early Hollywood first found its audience among immigrant populations in the United States. But, within a few years, that audience had become global. This shift occurred as the movies themselves were being transformed from the simple one-reelers to the more complex feature-length productions. The new audience cut across demographic lines, largely transcending differentiation by age, locale (urban or rural), gender, social class, and even nationality. I say *even* nationality because, on the heels of a war fought in the name of competing nationalisms and in spite of nationalist extremism in many countries in its wake, the global appeal of Hollywood triumphed.

Much theory and criticism of film contends that movies are a product and function of distinct, national cultures,[4] but from early on Hollywood's product and practice transcended national cultural norms. There were no national cultural traditions in the media arts, and that singularly distinctive cultural mode, language, was absent in the silent era. Even with the coming of sound in 1927, although there were initial technical problems to solve, little stood in the way of the "talkies" moving smoothly across national borders. The dubbing of different language tracks proved simple and, when deemed desirable, printed subtitles have served as substitutes. Viewers never have had problems with Humphrey Bogart, John Wayne, or Doris Day speaking German, a Spanish language version of *Baywatch*, or J. R. Ewing, Murphy Brown, and Dr. Peter Denton speaking Japanese. Since the end of the First World War, Hollywood's domination of the international market for movies essentially has remained uncontested. Despite all kinds of quotas on the import of Hollywood films or similar attempts to limit access to markets, and in spite of the Second World War, the Cold War, and myriad trade wars, nowhere has Hollywood been held back for long. The successes of any of the national cinemas competing against Hollywood have proven to be fleeting and problematic.

Moreover, Hollywood has always been willing to employ talent from all over the globe. German expressionist directors were lured to Hollywood in the twenties; exiles from Nazi Europe, World War Two, and Soviet-dominated Eastern Europe made careers in Hollywood; British artistic and technical talent found especially easy access to the industry; of late, an Australian director like Peter Weir or a German like Wolfgang Pertersen or a Frenchman like Luc Besson may toil in Hollywood alongside an Israeli-born producer like Menachem Golan or the Italian-born Dino DeLaurentis. The Oscars seem an essentially Hollywood idea, but the competition for them has been international since their inception.

Over time, many countries, including France, Germany, and Great Britain, enacted laws to limit the importation of Hollywood movies. Such laws established quota systems based on a ratio of the nationally produced movies to the number of Hollywood imports allowed. None of these restrictions proved to be effective. Part of this ineffectiveness could be attributed to the success of Hollywood producers in setting up affiliated companies in other countries and producing and/or distributing movies through these subsidiaries. On top of that, movies are a product that can be easily doctored or reedited.

The failure of these movie quota laws normally is attributed to the widespread presence of Hollywood subsidiaries in other countries and the cleverness of schemes intended to circumvent the quota laws. Looking at the history of these laws in various locales, however, I come to a different conclusion. Given the popular taste and the market for movies, there never has been a real national consensus anywhere that supports such quota laws against Hollywood movies. Even the movie industry in any given country has proven to be divided between its branches on this issue. The producing branch has favored laws and quotas to keep out Hollywood movies as a form of protectionism for native filmmakers. Distributors and exhibitors, on the other hand, have most often opposed such legislation because the market for Hollywood movies is so well established in so many populations.

Our received models of culture are national and literary. The technologies and arts of global communication, however, have entirely outstripped these models. The change can be seen in the spread of popular music that appeals to a global youth market and the rise of the golden arches of McDonald's on all the world's continents. Jeans, T-shirts, and baseball caps are worn by nearly anybody nearly anywhere. At first glance much of this looks like Americanization. Upon deeper examination, it doesn't. As recently as the late 1970s, even in the capitals of Western Europe, it still was difficult to find a good hamburger or to wear blue jeans to the theatre. All that has changed. By the same token, in the late 1970s it still was difficult to find imported beers and wines, much less anything in the way of breads and cheeses or a selection of different coffees in Bozeman, Montana. If you live in Paris, France you never have to go to McDonald's. If you live in Bozeman, Montana you never have to buy a bottle of wine from France. Both options now are so readily available in both places and in such abundance, however, that no one in either place gives any real thought to the matter anymore. The McDonald's on the Champs Elysées and the shops in Bozeman, Montana specializing in imported wines and cheeses are opposite sides of the same coin.

Early in the twentieth century, the establishment of the movies as international entertainment hearkened an enormous shift in the parameters of cultural experience. No longer did it matter where you lived; you could now see drama or comedy inexpensively and nearly anywhere that previously had been limited to live performances. No longer was artistic experience a function of elitism, whether economic, social, or educational. No longer was culture to be primarily determined nationally. With the movies artistic culture became accessible, exportable, and transferable in ways it had never been before. The globalization and democratization of culture was pioneered by Hollywood.

Television on the eve of the twenty-first century is global to an extent that the movies only dimly foreshadowed. Such sweeping change means many things, not the least of which must be a vast reappraisal of what we consider cultural and artistic experience to be. We are on the verge of enormous changes in our attitudes toward art and culture, even though these changes are largely still resisted by educators, critics, and journalists everywhere.

Through most of the twentieth century it has proven at least plausible for critics to attribute Hollywood's dominant influence in motion picture production, distribution, and exhibition around the world to the apparatus of capitalist exploitation marshaled in the service of American cultural imperialism. This explanation is problematic enough, however, since even in countries where there has been an American military presence for a half a century, like Germany or South Korea, the troops have not been forcing native populations to see American-made movies or television programs against their will. Popular movies, music, and television have spread like wildfire internationally to the inevitable enthusiastic response of younger audiences no matter what arguments and prohibitions their parents, teachers, and local authorities used to oppose them. But the truly convincing evidence on this score is that television, which has functioned as a broadcast system within national boundaries and under national governmental ownership or regulation everywhere, has developed so similarly around the globe. The taste for television is quite simply an undifferentiated global taste. No society has successfully prevented television from spreading in acceptance and popularity. No culture has developed forms of television that are genuinely distinct or national.

Since the 1970s television has caught on everywhere and is proving to be similar in its content and structure around the globe. What often has been attributed to Americanization turns out to be common, popular taste that is shared and imitated worldwide. This common taste has little to do with the domination of one national culture over another. In a 1994 book, Ohio University Professor Anne Cooper-Chen documents the apparently endless international fascination with game shows on TV around the world.[5] Many of these shows are not imported from the United States, but rather are clones of the game show formulas that originated on American television but which have been adapted to local circumstances. Cooper-Chen's research further reveals that television everywhere is dominated by similar types of entertainment programming.

The reality of common popular taste around the globe undermines a vast array of received ideas about art and culture. Mandela voters in one of South Africa's impoverished black townships are unlikely to show much enthusiasm toward a cultural policy that subsidizes the Johannesburg Symphony or that sponsors a traveling troupe performing plays by Bertolt Brecht, even though they may be open to Brecht's message of economic and social equality. They prefer to have a satellite dish in front of every dwelling. And what they want to receive on their TV sets is the well-established range of programming increasingly common throughout the world: sports, broadcast live with narration by experts and former athletes; news, tersely delivered by photogenic commentators, accompanied by vivid, often graphic, and swiftly edited footage of events; episodic comedies featuring characters who appear weekly enmeshed in slightly implausible, lighthearted domestic conflicts; action-oriented dramas presenting conflicts between characters that can be resolved convincingly in a short time; documentaries dealing with distant places or with nature. Alas, just such a menu consists of precisely the television fare that is seen everywhere.

That so many TV series from the United States are popular worldwide looks akin to the way Hollywood movies have dominated the big screens of movie theaters around the globe. Many commentators conclude that this phenomenon is explainable strictly as an instance of a rich and powerful producing nation imposing upon others its cultural product in colonial fashion. But then how is the popularity of native-produced programming that copies American models, like the scores of different versions of *The Wheel of Fortune*, *The Price is Right*, and *The Dating Game*, to be explained?[6] This is not the case of one dominant country exercising its cultural colonialism. Rather, models that first appeared in the United States are being taken over by television producers and programmers throughout the world. Such taking over of ideas may not necessarily even contribute to the direct profits of commercial interests in the United States that may earn nothing from French or Japanese news programs produced with techniques of reporting, camera work, and editing that first appeared in the United States, or from an Italian or a Filipino TV game show that resembles an American program. It is furthermore important to recognize that the commonality of taste for television around the globe constitutes a direct challenge to long held views about art and culture being determined nationally.

After my lecture in Dunkerque, I visited Paris for several days. In the French capital one afternoon I visited the famous cemetery in the northeast part of the city called Père Lachaise. Alongside common citizens, this is the final resting place of an exceptional number of important artists, philosophers, and politicians from Molière to Émile Zola, Louis Pasteur to Gertrude Stein, Guillaume Apollinaire to Talleyrand, Jean-Auguste Ingres to Georges Seurat, Georges Méliés to Simone Signoret, and Oscar Wilde. The cemetery is large and contains notable historic sites. In one corner is the infamous wall where leftist communards were executed in 1871 when their uprising was suppressed at the end of the Franco-Prussian War. But among all these historic spots and the remains of so many luminaries, only one grave in Père Lachaise is steadily inundated by visitors. Their numbers require that police guards be posted at that grave around-the-clock. Anyone gets an immediate sense of the special nature of this site upon first seeing any of the graffiti in the cemetery pointing the way to it. Written in various languages, some of them non-Western, the extent of this graffiti itself underscores the size of the crowds heading in the direction of this one grave. It is that of the American musician of the rock group The Doors who died in 1971 in a Paris hotel of an apparent drug overdose, Jim Morrison.

The continuing popularity of the pilgrimage to Morrison's tomb is no direct function of capitalist exploitation or cultural colonialism. No one owns a concession at the Morrison tomb. Profiteering record companies are not peddling CDs and cassettes in the shadow of his grave marker. There are no golden arches near Père Lachaise bidding the weary mourner to down a Big Mac or to quaff a Coca-Cola. The visitors to Jim Morrison's grave are there because of a widely shared interest among them for paying their respects to this tragic hero of rock music and the golden age of a youth counterculture that fleetingly appeared at the end of the 1960s.

Nor do many of the visitors to Morrison's tomb have much interest in the cemetery's other graves. Considered alongside this indifference toward visiting the graves of so many great figures of letters, science, and politics, what I am describing flies in the face of many traditional ideas about civilization and culture. At the same time, this adulation of Jim Morrison also flies in the face of much common wisdom that holds that the shared passion for popular culture is the result of an equation based solely upon the finely tuned exploitation of sounds, images, stories and personalities for direct economic gain.

The globalization of culture is widely and deeply resented by critics on both the ideological Left and the Right. The Left's dismay with popular culture is based on criticism of manipulation of the market place and the presumed victimization of audiences by profiteering manufacturers and distributors. Although the Cold War proper has ended, leftist contempt and hostility toward this co-optation of culture worldwide by what are considered to be exploitative American interests remain strong. By contrast, the Right criticizes popular culture because it is loose and self-indulgent, undermines authority and tradition, and casts historic notions of the good, the beautiful, and the true into disarray. The Right holds popular culture in contempt, not because of the economics on which its triumph is based, but because its results constitute a diminution of time-honored artifacts, practices, and values.

A critic of the media in the United States who can be identified as being on the Christian Right can sound just as vehement toward the cultural barbarism and exploitativeness of Hollywood movies and American television as did any communist in Eastern Europe before the end of the Cold War. Some leftist French intellectuals try to keep Hollywood movies and television shows produced in the United States from both the big screens and the small screens of their nation with a zeal equal to Islamic fundamentalists in Iran. The idea of preservation and protection, whether it be of national cultural prerogatives or of internationalist ideology, remains strong.

NOTES

1. Samuel H. Wilson, "Disney Dissonance," *Natural History*, December, 1994, p. 26; Martin Walker, "Disney's Saccharin Turns Sour," *World Press Review*, March, 1994, pp. 36, 37.

2. "Euro-Disney '93: $901 Million Loss," *The New York Times*, November 11, 1993, p. D4; also, Jolie Solomon, "Mickey's Trip to Trouble," *Newsweek*, February 14, 1994, pp. 34-37.

3. See, Neal Gabler, *An Empire of Their Own: How the Jews Invented Hollywood* (New York: Crown Publishers, 1988).

4. See, Paul Monaco, *Cinema & Society: France & Germany During the Twenties* (New York/Amsterdam: Elsevier, 1976), Chapters 2 & 3, and passim.

5. Anne Cooper-Chen, *Games in the Global Village: A 50-Nation Study of Entertainment Television* (Bowling Green, OH: Bowling Green University Press, 1994).

6. Michael Logan, "Wheel of Fortune Sends in the Clones," *TV Guide*, October 26 - November 1, 1991, p. 15.

6

Wellsprings of Our Discontent with Television

Criticisms of television have been woven together into a tight package of received ideas about the "dangers" of this medium since the 1960s. The sources of these suspicions about television are many, and the ideas upon which they are based have been repeatedly refined. In this chapter, I have selected four figures whose thinking has been seminal in forming the societal and cultural fears that are widely expressed toward television.

In 1964, a Canadian professor named Marshall McLuhan published a bestseller entitled *Understanding Media: The Extensions of Man.* The volume consisted of a series of essays in which McLuhan declared television to be a "cool medium," differentiating it from both print and film. "The film image," he wrote, "offers many more millions of data per second, and the viewer does not have to make the same drastic reduction of items to form his impression. He tends instead to accept the full image as a package deal. In contrast, the viewer of the TV mosaic with technical control of the image, unconsciously reconfigures the dots into an abstract work of art on the pattern of a Seurat or Rouault."[1]

Just over a decade before McLuhan's *Understanding Media* was published, on a summer afternoon in 1953, my grandmother took me to a movie matinee at the Palace Theater in Albany, New York. It was a memorable occasion. The movie was a western and it was in 3-D! I recall neither the movie's title nor the actual process of putting on the plastic glasses that I had to wear to watch it. I do remember that the plastic glasses had to be returned in the lobby after the movie was over. What I still have clear in my memory was the scene of a barroom brawl when everybody in the audience ducked as a stool was thrown right toward us. My mind's ear still remembers the shrieks that went up that afternoon from the couple of hundred people in the Palace. Today, however, 3-D lingers primarily in the collective memory as a point of humorous reference for Hollywood's failed experiment. Nonetheless, it is precisely the failure of 3-D that reveals something fundamental and important about the movies and TV.

One view holds that 3-D failed for reasons of hygiene because audiences resisted the idea of sharing the reusable plastic glasses. Another argues that Hollywood steered away from developing 3-D because of its expense. The first notion seems fanciful. The glasses weren't expensive to manufacture and, had 3-D caught on, an entrepreneur surely would have come up with personal 3-D glasses that you could own and take with you to the movies. The second may be more plausible, although Hollywood rarely has resisted spending money when the major studios are convinced that even bigger profits can be made. The best explanation is that audiences did not perceive themselves as needing or wanting 3-D. If they had, the technology would have become widespread, sooner or later.

Indeed, the failure of 3-D movies points toward an abiding flaw in McLuhan's celebrated attempt to describe and define television by analysis of the particular nature of the medium's picture. In *Understanding Media* McLuhan declared that "it is hard for literate people, with their habits of fixed points of view and three-dimensional vision, to understand the properties of two-dimensional vision."[2] Even for Marshall McLuhan this was quite a mouthful, leaving one to wonder just what in the world he was talking about. The photograph, the motion picture, and television all present flattened two-dimensional pictures that are not resisted by viewers at all! In fact, the popular rejection of 3-D in the 1950s reinforces the idea that the look of three-dimensionality is a visual element about which viewers do not much care.

McLuhan's assumption that television was what he labeled a "cool medium" was based entirely upon his false observations about the uniqueness and primacy of the mosaic-like picture transmitted by television. From precisely that mistake, moreover, McLuhan easily slipped over into one of his broadest claims about the social and cultural influences of the medium, which he phrased in a single sentence: "TV is a medium that rejects the sharp personality and favors the presentation of processes rather than of products."[3]

To a startling degree, McLuhan's opinions gained currency and still prevail under the guise of unchallengeable truths about television. McLuhan himself proceeded from his proclamation of TV as a cool medium to even more ambitious conclusions about the relationship of television to politics that remain unproven but which are widely accepted. He offered, for example, an interpretation of Richard Nixon's 1963 appearance on NBC's *Tonight Show*, arguing that by playing the piano on that program Nixon had demonstrated a side to his personality that voters had not seen during the 1960 election. Had that side of Nixon come through, McLuhan claimed, he would have beaten John F. Kennedy at the polls.[4] This stab at electoral analysis by McLuhan still stands at the heart of continuing claims that television has ushered in a new and wholly capricious era in politics.

In his assessment of the 1960 election, however, McLuhan ignored the complexities of history and the political process. He presented a model of reductionist determinism that media studies and critiques of television subsequently have readily endorsed, even though the basis for McLuhan's claims were so weak. After all, long after his TV appearance on *The Tonight Show* in 1963 Richard Nixon still was called "Tricky Dick," still was widely perceived as an upwardly mobile middle class stiff, and still was widely seen as someone who had eagerly and excessively exploited Cold War anti-communism. In the eyes of many citizens and much of the media, even after he tickled the ivories on a TV talk show, he was still a man whose pedestrian credentials had been redeemed only by President Dwight Eisenhower's happenstance acceptance of him as a vice-presidential running mate in 1952. Still, Nixon survived all this and won election to the Presidency in 1968 and reelection to it in 1972. Had he done enough piano playing stints on the tube in the interim to truly reconstruct his image? Were his political ads suddenly ready for prime time? Had enough pancake make up been applied to his visage to cover the traces of five o'clock shadow? Was this politician who was presumably unmade by television during the 1960 presidential election campaign subsequently remade by it before the end of the decade?

Much of the educated and informed world, four decades later, still will maintain that Kennedy's beating Nixon in the 1960 election was caused by television. More importantly, McLuhan's speculation about the 1960 presidential election created a causal scenario linking television appearance and electoral success that has been molded into a model claiming to explain the medium's entire relationship to the political process. Never mind all the other causal explanations for Kennedy's win or all the various factors that might have influenced his precariously slim margin of victory in the popular vote. McLuhan's central idea prevails: television favors personalities over processes (whatever that means) and personality type will henceforth determine politics in nefarious ways.

Marshall McLuhan's speculations about television have remained widespread and influential. It is widely believed that TV's advent has altered political culture and that only "cool" masters of the medium will dominate public life in the future. Since television itself is defined by the peculiarity of the picture transmitted on it, the medium becomes the message. Many of McLuhan's phrases were catchy, and some, like "the global village," have endured quite well. But McLuhan misunderstood what TV was. He distorted television's impact upon culture and society by assuming that the particular visual characteristics of the TV picture were capable of altering human consciousness.

By the late 1960s, Marshall McLuhan had become an enormously popular figure. A man who achieved less celebrity, but whose influence on the way we have come to think about television was as great as McLuhan's was the Stanford University psychologist Albert Bandura. Bandura was not interested primarily in the media and their effects. As a psychologist exploring learning and behavior, he conducted a number of pioneering experiments. Part of this research continues to provide a model for how society explains and accounts for what are believed to be the negative influences of television, especially on children. In a book published in 1963, Bandura summarized his interpretation of the initial stages of the research that he and others had begun conducting in the 1950s: "Pictorially presented models are provided in films, television, and other audiovisual displays. . . . Because of the amount of time during which most young people are exposed to pictorially presented models, mainly through television . . . such models play a major part in shaping behavior." [5] To be sure, Bandura's conclusions were supported by a number of psychologists and other social scientists at the time and they subsequently have attracted widespread endorsement in learned circles. The problem is that all these subsequent experiments, observations, and interpretations really have not added up to what has been claimed. The long-term effects of exposure to specific pictorial material upon behavior remains unproven.

Typically, Bandura conducted experiments in which children were

shown a film of an adult acting aggressively toward an inflatable doll–
someone using a rubber mallet to hit a doll that looks like a clown or
someone punching the doll. As the film proceeded, this punching became
more agitated and violent, and the blows increased in their frequency.
Finally, the inflatable doll was knocked repeatedly to the floor. Then,
children who had seen this film were presented with a similar inflated
doll, and they were given rubber mallets. Lo and behold, they imitated
what they had seen in the film. They went to work beating up the doll.[6]
Alternatively, Bandura and other researchers demonstrated their
hypothesis by showing children animated cartoons. After watching
them, the children were allowed to play and frequently behaviors
portrayed in the cartoon, including aggressive ones, were mimicked by
them.

But just what do such experiments really demonstrate? What insights
can be carried over from the universities where such experiments are
conducted to real life? Are we justified in saying that such experiments
prove that media presentations provoke aggression and violence? Make
no mistake, the theory of imitation that is derived from just such research
fuels the common idea that films and television are potent sources for
negative behaviors. The questionable leap, however, is from the data of
an experimental situation in which such immediate imitative behavior is
observed to the notion that such effects are widespread over time in
society and produce specific aggressive and asocial behaviors.

Watching a film and then being invited to imitate an action shown
in it cannot prove that humans actually behave as they do because of
media influence. But this is just the leap that our culture has made in its
collective thinking. It is as if one of the most popularly held ideas in our
society maintains: You are whatever you see and hear! If it is on the
screen, it will be imitated. This is not just a short-term problem. What
has been seen and heard necessarily will be replicated in some precise
way in behavior and come back to haunt us all. So, count up the
instances of violence portrayed in the media's fictional stories and you
will be able to account for the assaults and murders on our streets.

As a society, we have been drawn way off base by following this line
of thinking. Movies and TV programs can make you angry, make you
cry, make you laugh until your sides hurt, or scare the pants off you. Such
short-term reactions among viewers, however, do not translate into long
term predictable effects on their behavior. During the summer of 1960,
when I was seventeen and had just graduated from high school, I went to

see the movie *Psycho* directed by Alfred Hitchcock. The next day I came home from my summer job hot and sweaty. Still thinking of the scene in that movie when the character played by Janet Leigh is stabbed to death in a shower, I showered with the bathroom door open. I recall the incident clearly. My grandmother, who lived with us, protested that this was bizarre and improper behavior. I was trying my best to be discreet, but still she found the open bathroom door to be an affront to the propriety of our home. Nonetheless, I had seen Janet Leigh's character get stabbed to death the night before on the big screen at the Palace Theater and I was taking no chances! I finished my shower with the door open.

   Psycho certainly put together a convincing set of shots of that murderous hand coming in on poor Ms. Leigh. I did not believe that the killer played by Anthony Perkins was actually lurking around our house in Albany, New York, but my better judgment was to take no undue risk. But that one shower also was the end of it! Much like the time, seven or eight years later, when I started one evening to read a paperback novel entitled *The Boston Strangler*. I became so engrossed in it and so fearful about what it described that I stayed awake on the sofa all night reading the book until daybreak; I was too scared to close my eyes and go to sleep alone in my apartment. But while any work of the imagination may so grip us, such reactions predict no long-term consequences. What we see in the movies or on television, like what we see on stage at a theatre performance, or hear at a concert, or see in a gallery or a museum, or read in the pages of a book, may move us. But because we are emotionally moved does not necessarily predict long term effects upon our behavior.

   The claims about media effects are based upon a specious model of human intelligence, reasoning, and development. In essence, claims about media effects have to endorse assumptions about learning that are tenuous and fallacious. After all, even when people are consciously trying to learn material the rate of their retention is strikingly low: measured at 10 percent for what normal subjects read, 20 percent for what is heard, and barely 30 percent for what is seen.[7] The notion that humans are slavishly imitating behaviors that they see in the movies or on television is laughable, except that it is taken so seriously.

   McLuhan thought that he had demonstrated rhetorically that television was powerful enough to subvert human consciousness. Bandura thought that he had demonstrated experimentally that media images provoked direct, imitative behaviors that were socially harmful. Whatever their deepest intentions, between the two of them, by the mid 1960s, the seeds had been sown to support the conclusion that television is socially and culturally disruptive and harmful. This was a rehash, in most ways, of claims about the negative effects of movies that had been advanced since the earliest years of the twentieth century. But the effects argument as it has been applied to television has been given far more credibility by intellectuals and found more enthusiasm among politicians because civilization could be made to appear facing devastation since television was available all the time and to be found in everyone's home.

In the context of examining claims about media effects, I have just finished rewatching a *Frontline* show that first aired on PBS early in 1995. The program was produced by Bill Moyers and concerns to what extent television effects viewers by influencing them toward violence. It raises basic questions about the assumed causal effects between TV content and asocial behaviors. As it turns out, in the upstate city of Hudson, New York, a study was begun many years earlier to trace the effects on children of watching large amounts television, including lots of violence. Tracking an individual over time, of course, is fundamental to what is needed to build a research case that might demonstrate the long-term effects of exposure to specific media programming as a child. Although even with such a long-term study, you would still need to factor in all sorts of variables over the decades to render the conclusion of such a study more defensible and compelling than is usually the case. How, after all, could you finally be absolutely certain that it was television that made your subject do something naughty and not the devil?

For their show, the *Frontline* staff located two adults who had been part of the original study and who had watched a lot of violent fare on TV as kids. One of them wound up abusing drugs and skirting dangerously with criminality. The program's producers find him living alone, marginally employed, and clearly unhappy. Across town, however, is the other man who soaked up equal amounts of violent fare on TV. Yet, as an adult, this second man appears to be a remarkably stable citizen. He is happily married, productively employed, with children of his own, and no record whatsoever of committing crimes, having scrapes with the law, or behaving asocially. In sum, the contemporary evidence points only to the conclusion that exposure to TV-violence is a wash! Some people who watched a lot of violence on TV as children may turn out badly. Others turn out fine. And certainly no one is arguing that the ones who turned out fine did so because as children they watched lots of violence on TV. Nonetheless, there is a nagging and underlying tone that pervades the PBS program. The suggestion keeps resurfacing that there *must* be a causal connection between violence on television and violence in real life. Even when the evidence points in the opposite direction, the show hesitates. So pervasive is the presumed causal link between exposure to violence on television and subsequent violent behavior that even when such a link is nowhere demonstrated, then surely we must be overlooking it.

All is not right with the world, and the world is full of TV. There *has* to be a connection between a TV diet rich in violence and the criminal or asocial behavior occurring in society–but try as they will to generate the evidence that will support this hypothesis, the producers keep coming up short. The causal links between early exposure to TV violence and asocial or criminal behavior later in life elude them completely. So, finally, a frustrated *Frontline* turns to Dr. George Gerbner of the Annenberg School of Communication at the University of Pennsylvania. A renowned researcher on the subject, Gerbner has authored numerous studies on television and violence over four decades, while sending out waves of well-prepared graduate students who have mastered the techniques, lingo, and lore of such investigation. Confronted by the program's nagging question as to why the producers' findings do not demonstrate the suspected links between TV and violence, Gerbner is able to assure viewers that media effects produce not so much behaviors as they do *contexts* for them. Television, he argues, cultivates an atmosphere of fear, intimidation, and a sense of victimization. As we keep on watching TV it fills us with loathing for what we think is going on outside in the streets. Maybe television does not really cause crime, Gerbner is suggesting, so much as exposure to it makes us feel endangered. Television's truly negative contribution to society, then, is that it fuels (false?) perceptions of abounding crime and evil in the world about us.

Many things, however, are coincidence. I am watching this *Frontline* program for a second time because I am to participate in a panel discussion on violence and the media that follows it. In the studio, before our discussion portion of the program begins, one of my fellow panelists remarks that it is a miracle that I do not seem to be suffering from jet lag. His comment is appropriate. I have just returned from accompanying my wife and thirteen honors students from Montana State

University on a two-week trip to Italy. I've been back in Montana less than a day. All went well, but in preparing for that trip we had read a good deal about being cautious in Italy for pickpockets and petty thievery. We carried our money in travelers' checks, wore money pouches under our clothes, stored passports and tickets in them, kept a keen eye on our luggage in rail stations, and locked our train compartments as we slept in berths hurtling through the night. Our cautions were based on warnings we found in the Harvard University Student Service's *Let's Go Italy*, and which were echoed in a British guidebook to Italy. We approached Italy knowing that in a country full of tourists, while violent crimes against one's person are rare, pick pockets, petty thievery, and the snatching of purses, cameras, and luggage are not.

We did not learn any of this from television! Since our return, however, I have seen one commercial spot on TV for American Express that portrays a noisy group of child pickpockets accosting a tourist and distracting him in a distinctively Italian-looking piazza. Initially, I concluded that our group's precautions in Italy were excessive; we had been overly cautious. But, then, three weeks after our return, I encountered a student who had spent a year abroad. After her stay in France, she and her companions had traveled in Italy. One night in the train she and her companions had money pouches cut off them and stolen as they slept.

On *Frontline*, along with Professor Gerbner's interview, there are intercuts of brief interviews with parents, several of whom are single mothers. They are asked whether they worry about their kids being exposed to too much violence, crime, and asocial behavior on television. "No!" they all say. In fact, they find TV to be a good companion for the children and consider their kids to be safer and healthier at home behind locked doors watching television than spending time outside on the streets of the neighborhood where they live.

There are urban neighborhoods in America that nearly all of us would avoid after dark, and some that many of us would steer clear of during the day as well. Contrary to George Gerbner's suggestions, what is the evidence that TV has driven us to paranoia and unreasoned judgments about crime? People possess rational concerns about crime and danger. They have various sources of information available to them upon which to base these assessments. Television is among them, but having lived in a city where my home was burglarized twice in the mid-1980s, I have no recollection of deciding that it had been broken into and plundered on any other basis than the first hand evidence of these occurrences. After the second burglary at that address, I bought and installed a security alarm system and the property has not been broken into since.

In recent years, along with a number of other scholars, Gerbner has established an approach to understanding the content analysis of television that is called *the cultivation perspective*. Applying it, Gerbner and others have explored what is called television's "mean world syndrome." At heart, this is what Gerbner is talking about in his interview with *Frontline*. Basically, this research assesses the responses of television viewers to questions such as, "Is greater 'protection' needed in society?" or "Can most people be trusted?" or "Are most people just looking out for themselves?" and attempts to correlate their answers to the program content that they prefer.

Perceiving the world as hostile and menacing is assumed *a priori* by this research to be a social ill, which, ostensibly, is attributable to the subject's television viewing patterns. Not surprisingly the researchers maintain that such studies demonstrate that the more people watch TV the more their negative view of the world has been cultivated. And, also, not surprisingly, as such studies do strive to be more current, today's researchers are careful to assess responses of the subjects in light of certain variables. For example, for persons categorized as either light or heavy TV viewers there is a considerable variable in their responses to the same questions when comparing college-educated respondents to those who never had attended college.[8]   In this kind of subtlety Gerbner's model of cultivation research appears comparable to Bandura's discovery of a difference between the ways boys and girls respond to aggressive behavior that they have seen on film in the earlier imitation studies. But in addition to such subtlety, Gerbner's research also shares with Bandura's a similar warp. For how can an experimenter be certain as to where, when, how, and why such attitudes as those found in the responses recorded in the "Mean World Syndrome" study truly originate? *All* the variables and possible influences cannot possibly be factored in. Isolating television as the cause of perceptions that are deemed by the experimenters to be inaccurate and undesirable is no more convincing than saying that film or television directly causes violent or aggressive behavior. And how, after all, do the researchers know just how mean the world really is or how can they claim to know the differences between caution and paranoia? There *are* dangerous and unpleasant places and situations, just as there are individuals and groups whose intentions are malevolent. The issue is not that the hours someone spends watching television cannot be quantified; obviously they can be. The problem is that no one can adequately qualify just how, and to what effect, that television watching was done.

When 100,000 people attend the annual Rose Bowl football game, some go home elated because their team won while fans of the losing team sulk over a dropped pass or a referee's lousy call. Some fans are happy because it was a day with lots of sunshine and a light breeze, so they got a great tan. Others may fret because they forgot a hat or their sun screen, and worry about having gotten too much sun. The scores of millions of Americans who watch professional football's annual Super Bowl on television are no different. Some are disappointed because it is another blow out and their team is on the losing end. Others can take interest and pleasure in watching the winning team strut its stuff, concentrating on just how well its players are performing. Still others see it simply as a pleasant way to spend a mid winter's Sunday afternoon and evening with friends while indulging in chips, chili, peanuts, and beer.

Humans are legitimately interested in what can be ordered, classified, and generalized about. To be able to do just these things is of value and necessity in our pursuit of the development of enlightened discourse and the progress of civilization. We deceive ourselves, however, if we fail to recognize that within all groups, classes, and categories, differences are individual. It is the failure of this recognition, in part, that accounts for much of our inability to correctly assess our changing society and culture, and television's place in it.

Neil Postman, a New York University professor of communication, holds to a premise that reformulates and advances McLuhan's maxim that the medium is the message. Postman argues this clearly when he writes that "the form in which ideas are expressed affects what those ideas will be."[9] But what exactly does this mean? If the statement referred only to the fact that different modes of presentation differ in their formal elements–delivering exactly the same words of this chapter as a public speech, for example–it would be one thing. Putting something into speech *is* different than putting it into print. The notion that the medium is the message and that ideas slavishly follow form in a deterministic manner, however, is an intellectual construct that is false.

To get a handle on Postman's insight into TV and politics, think your way through this argument, for example. He maintains that "it is implausible to imagine that anyone like our twenty-seventh President [of the United States], the multi-chinned, three-hundred pound William Howard Taft, could be put forward as a presidential candidate in today's world."[10] Such a statement, at first glance, is tough to argue with. William Howard Taft possessed a pretty unique body type no matter what the era and no matter what the mode of communication that was considered dominant during it! Postman's suggestion that we won't see Taft's likeness making a stab at the White House anytime soon seems reasonably plausible.

But, for argument's sake, if Neil Postman took a look across the Atlantic at Chancellor Helmut Kohl of Germany he would find, indeed, a world leader whose weight pushes 300 pounds. For years Kohl's political opponents–and likely many of his supporters as well–have referred to him unflatteringly as "the Pear" (Die Birne). This is a reference to the fact that the chancellor's average sized head is situated atop a massive body that bulges uncompromisingly in the mid and lower sections.

I have seen Helmut Kohl in the flesh. He is one massive man. President Bill Clinton once remarked that he'd been watching *two* Sumo wrestlers on TV the night before and was reminded of Chancellor Kohl. Nonetheless, Kohl has the record for holding the office of chancellor for the longest period of time in German history, and he has led that country through challenging times, including its reunification in the early 1990s. Moreover, Germany is one of a few nations in which the percentage of residences receiving television actually tops the United States; over ninety-nine percent of the dwellings in Germany have at least one TV set.

Without an enormous amount of cross-cultural and historical data how could we ever convincingly conclude that television has created a political culture demanding more photogenic and conventionally attractive candidates? And, even if there were evidence of "better-looking" of more physically fit candidates, how could we be certain that television caused this phenomenon? Why not say that Americans are not likely to vote for 300-pound candidates because the population increasingly has become health conscious and many of us might believe that obesity reflects unhealthy behavior rooted in character flaws? Like McLuhan's, Postman's model of how TV influences the electorate is narrow and deterministic. His fundamental idea is that the relationship between an image and its effect is causal, and that the public responds politically to image alone. It is not entirely clear, however, just how Postman and others like him manage to rise above this seduction while the rest of us are its victims.

More importantly, Postman reveals the real ideological drive behind his criticism of television when he argues that television in democratic free-market societies is akin to the apparatus of centralized government in totalitarian states. To get to this point, Postman interestingly chooses to quote from a speech by George Gerbner:

"Television is the new state religion run by a private Ministry of Culture (the three networks), offering a universal curriculum for all people, financed by a form of hidden taxation without representation. You pay when you wash, and not when you watch."[11]

Gerbner makes clear that he doesn't like television paid for by advertisers. Does he dislike such TV because it is inherently flawed or because it depends on capitalist investors who have the means to underwrite television's costly productions with their payments for advertising? Does he dislike such TV because it functions within a market economy, and he prefers another economic system?

Gerbner and Postman point us toward the deep and underlying issues that are at stake in the contemporary criticism of television. If we are asking seriously what TV is, why television has become the presence around the globe that it is, and if we inquire as to where the bulk of most contemporary criticism of television leads, these questions follow:

"What kind of an economic order do you wish to live in?"
"How do you view and interpret competition between people and between ideas?"
"What is your view of individual responsibility and choice?"
"Do you assess a market system as being injurious to a healthy civil order and the culture that grows within it?"
"Are you willing to see society and culture be free so that both may develop organically out of the competing ideas, stories, beliefs, and images within them?"

Postman makes clear his own views on such matters, dragging along Gerbner in his wake:

"I believe he [Gerbner] means to say—and, in any case, *I* do—that in the Age of

Television . . . we have less to fear from government restraints than from television glut; that in fact, we have no way of protecting ourselves from information being disseminated by corporate America."[12]

Here we are then! The real problem is that television is part of that evil monolith called corporate America that Postman perceives as single-mindedly pumping images, sounds, dramas, sitcoms, sports, news, public affairs, and talk shows into an anesthetized public. Getting to the heart of his argument that television victimizes us all, Postman concludes that "we have no way of protecting ourselves from information disseminated [on TV]."[13]

But can anyone seriously argue that Pat Robertson's *700 Club*, *Murphy Brown*, *Hard Copy*, *N.Y.P.D. Blue*, ABC's *Monday Night Football*, MTV's *Singled Out*, Court-TV, a natural history documentary on the Discovery Channel, or a classic movie channel are the same "universal curriculum" (Gerbner) and "information disseminated" (Postman)? Are we to believe that some single, monolithic entity called corporate America is orchestrating the entire range of TV programming as a unified assault upon human sensibility? Such a line of thinking has nothing to do with the realities of the artistic, economic, cultural, and societal complexities of television at the dawn of the twenty-first century.

NOTES

1. Marshall, McLuhan, *Understanding Media: The Extensions of Man* (New York: Signet Books, 1964), p. 269.

2. ibid., p. 273.

3. ibid., p. 269.

4. ibid., p. 269.

5. Albert Bandura and Richard H. Walters, *Social Learning and Personality Development* (New York: Holt, Rinehart, and Winston, Inc., 1963), p. 49.

6. ibid., pp. 60-67.

7. Michael W. Cronin, "Oral Communication Across the Curriculum ," Seminar, Montana State University, Bozeman, May 12, 1997.

8. Jennings Bryant and Dolf Zillmans, eds., *Media Effects: Advances in Theory and Research* (Hillsdale, NJ: L. Erlbaum Associates, 1994), p. 31.

9. Neil Postman, *Amusing Ourselves to Death: Public Discourse in the Age of Show Business* (New York/London: Penguin USA, 1986), p. 9.

10. ibid., p. 33. This idea did not originate with McLuhan, by the way, but with Yale University history professor David M. Potter. *Variety*, July 27, 1960, reported Potter's address to students at McAlaster College in Minneapolis. In it, he contended that American Presidents Cleveland, Taft, and Coolidge all would have been considered too unimpressive in front of TV-cameras to even be nominated by their parties. Potter, though, apparently never perpetuated this idea into the kind of "gospel truth" that McLuhan and Postman subsequently did.

11. ibid., p. 140.

12. ibid., p. 140.

13. ibid., p. 140.

7

Television and Advertising

McLuhan, Bandura, Gerbner, and Postman all have contributed significantly to how our culture commonly regards television. They provide perspectives that are basic to the contemporary criticism of this medium. It would not, however, be difficult to come up with the names of scores of other prominent thinkers and writers who hold ideas similar to theirs. At its heart, negative criticism of television is based upon the notion that humans are rendered helpless and hapless before the TV set. Television is perceived as powerful, hypnotic, and addictive. Television will hook you and hold you. The machine and its technology are capable of undermining our critical faculties. Hence, TV reigns havoc upon society and culture at large, and our relationship to TV is perilous. But this entire line of thinking poses a fundamental question: Are we really TV's victims, or has television simply become the handiest of scapegoats for contemporary cultural criticism?

The prevailing model for interpreting television's relationship to its audience is one in which viewers are defenseless. But this line of thinking ignores the complexity of anyone's relationship to whatever he or she sees and hears. The dynamic between any media and its audience is quite complex. To unravel that dynamic, let us focus on that form of communication in which a message is aimed directly toward a target audience, namely advertising.

All advertising demonstrates several characteristics, including being dependent upon repetition. The short length of advertising spots means not only that they come and go rapidly, but also that they are available to be repeated again and again. For now, however, I want to draw your attention to a dimension of advertising having nothing to do with repetition per se. That fundamental issue is the *positioning* of any viewer in relationship specifically to the meaning and value of any particular advertisement

During most of my adult life, I have enjoyed drinking beer. I like it in all seasons, at various social occasions, and with a variety of foods. As I have grown older, I have realized that, although liking the taste of beer I would prefer to be able to drink it, on many occasions, without the presence of the alcohol brewed into it. Some time ago, then, I was pleased to see a television advertisement for a nonalcoholic beer that promised full flavor. While reserving some skepticism toward the idea that it would taste like real beer to me, I decided to try it. The next day I was in a restaurant, ordering lunch, and asked the waitress for a nonalcoholic beer by name, O'Doul's. That was the product I had seen advertised on TV the night before. But the waitress responded that the establishment did not carry O'Doul's. Would I like to try, she wondered, a Sharp's instead? I proceeded to order, purchase, and consume only Sharp's nonalcoholic beer for the next several years, when another coincidence caused me to change brands. An establishment was out of Sharp's and I had a Coor's Cutter, the taste of which I preferred.

From the point of view of O'Doul's, the original advertiser whose product had been presented to me on TV, the result was a bust! I had chosen a competitor's brew over it, stuck with that for quite a while, and, then, when I changed, chose yet another competitor's product. Statistically, of course, the Anheuser-Busch company that produces O'Doul's, as well as its advertising agency, could argue that what I am describing was happenstance. They would maintain that most viewers of the ad who responded to it at all wound up trying O'Doul's. Some number of those who tried it would continue to buy O'Doul's as the commercial intended. Nonetheless, this incident raises fundamental questions as to the receptivity, interest, inclination, and reaction of any individual to a specific advertisement.

Let me offer one other illustration. A number of years ago I was diagnosed as diabetic. I use insulin to regulate this condition, and, on the advice of a physician and a dietitian, I have cut back substantially on the sugar that I eat. Hence, I have become a person with no interest in advertisements for products containing sugar. Conversely, I am now a good target for products containing artificial sweeteners, which I never was before. Until I was diagnosed with diabetes, I had eaten refined sugar regularly and probably sought to avoid it less than the average middle-aged American. Now when I see a commercial for regular Coca-Cola it holds no interest for me, but I do want to know about drinks on the market that are flavored with artificial sweeteners.

All media is targeted at specific interests and tastes. Advertisers, media producers, and programmers assess with whom their products might find positive response by judging audience demographics. Profiles of people by age, income, gender, marital status, and region define promising audiences for specific advertisements, just as they do for shows on television or for movies at a theater. For myself, my friends, and the colleagues with whom I teach, automobile commercials for a Lexus, an Acura, or a Mercedes are a loss. These vehicles are priced beyond our reasonable and likely consideration. Lost on us, too, are commercials for "low-end" vehicles such as Geos. These are considered too small, too light, too uncomfortable, or too cheap for the middle-aged, middle-income buyers like myself.

The situation of the viewer determines the effectiveness of all media, and all media function according to this basic standard. In contemporary culture, however, there is a tendency to argue that advertising creates needs. This assumption is based upon the notion that genuine needs are readily distinguished from capricious ones. On what premise, however, can we conclude that a particular buyer does not *need* a large American automobile with oversized tires, a low-riding chassis, and a shiny metallic paint job? For an unmarried twenty-four-year-old construction worker this "muscle car" makes as much sense as does a Volvo station wagon for a forty-four-year-old insurance executive, married with two children.

Any successful economy strives toward abundance and diversity, which in affluent democracies can only result in ever-widening consumer choices. Rationality and need as economic values can be determined only by individuals assessing their own circumstances. It makes as much sense for one person to spend money buying a T-shirt with the likeness of a popular rock musician on it as it does for another to make a cash donation to the local symphony orchestra. Dining at an elegant restaurant is not a more rational choice than picking up a pizza at a nationally advertised fast food outlet. My diabetic need to avoid sugar exists before any advertising that I see for drinks that are sweetened with sugar substitutes.

Much of the cultural criticism of film, video, and television in the United States thrives because these media function as part of a competitive market system. Critics of the market system are convinced that there are rational and ethical grounds for distinguishing between what they call *real* needs and artificial ones. Such criticism holds advertising to be particularly culpable for what are perceived to be its capricious and invidious appeals. Some advertising, of course, speaks only to the simple need for a product or a service. I have to buy *something* to wash my clothes, and any soap or detergent will likely get them clean. Other products and services, however, are advertised on the basis of appealing to more complex desires such as being attractive or having status. Basic needs of shelter, food, and clothing, however, always can be satisfied at minimal levels. Any desires beyond them, or any elaborations upon those desires, may be deemed *unnecessary*. All these unnecessary products and services, moreover, can be distinguished from one another only on the basis of taste.

With regard to the criticism of television, substantial numbers of us distrust our fellow citizens. Specifically, we distrust differences of taste, and we assume that because others like what we do not like that their tastes point toward undesirable social and behavioral consequences. Hence, we postulate crude and undemonstrated parallels between taste and both public and private behavior, and we speculate wildly on what we believe will be the results of other people liking what we do not like.

Is it not odd that claims of the pernicious and manipulative influences of television inevitably point to fears about someone else's viewing and behavior? *We* can see through offensive programming. *We* do not watch the wrong shows, or, if we do, we manage not to be taken in by their violence, sensationalism, perversity, crudity, and shallowness. Are we really convinced that all the cultural critics who debunk popular taste and advertising are simply too attractive and of too high a social status to be drawn in by such appeals? What makes us so certain that we can avoid the pitfalls of bad taste, media manipulation, and advertising appeals while others cannot? In any number of spheres, a considerable number of Americans repeatedly fall back upon the odd notion that their fellow citizens cannot make sound choices about their own needs and desires. Hence, our cultural assessment of popularity usually is in direct proportion to how it relates to our own taste. It is an all-too-familiar feeling, is it not, to shake one's head in dismay when what we dislike becomes popular? Conversely, we nod in enthusiastic agreement when the masses see things our way! Popularity is a comfortable notion so long as it corresponds to our own tastes and is a very disturbing one when it does not.

The resonance between an advertisement, a news report, or a fictional story and any given viewer is only speculatively explainable. This is because responsiveness resides with the individual, a fact that almost all the models of analysis that claim to explain contemporary culture either ignore or minimize. And individual responsiveness is fickle! Even given the sophistication of the producers and marketers of media fare, the media business is not an especially easy one. Popular programs come and go; advertising pitches flop or peter out; a potential blockbuster movie, appearing to have all the makings of a hit, goes bust; sensational or incriminating news stories never catch on with the public; a TV show's ratings are good for several years and then plummet.

In spite of all the evidence to the contrary, there still remains a strong belief that film and television are powerful, manipulative, and capable of undermining human judgment while reeking havoc upon civilization. Critics remain convinced that advertising forces us to buy products and services for which we have no genuine need and that life itself is being reduced to an ugly treadmill of consumption. They also argue that advertising threatens the American Republic at the very center of its public institutions, because the political process itself is being undermined by television spots.

The presidency of Ronald Reagan, 1981-1989, was deeply criticized by much of America's intellectual establishment and its political successes were largely attributed to media manipulation. The fact that Reagan was a former actor provided *prima facie* evidence that mastery over the media must be his only message. Quite aside was the fact that his acting career lay more than two decades behind him and that he had served ably as the governor of California for two terms. The Reagan presidency still was widely treated as constituting the dubious reign of the great communicator whose media savvy and personal guile combined to dupe the nation into eight years of collective amnesia. Reagan was assailed as the "teflon president" and widely held responsible by much of the media and in academic circles for accelerating the deterioration of serious public discourse in favor of media imagery and manipulation.

Toward the end of the Reagan presidency in 1988 a political spot was aired on television by the campaign of his vice president and successor George Bush. The notorious "Willie Horton" ad is claimed to mark a low point for manipulative and negative campaigning. It criticized a parole release program under the Democrats' presidential candidate, Michael Dukakis, while he was Governor of the Commonwealth of Massachusetts. While on furlough from one of the Bay State's correctional facilities, Horton fled to Maryland where he raped and murdered a woman.

The Willie Horton political spot is short and graphic. Does it misrepresent what occurred? In the brief time that the ad runs, larger and complex questions about how it is to be interpreted are not addressed. A viewer might wonder, for example, to what extent former Governor Dukakis personally was responsible for the furlough program. It would be informative to know in how many cases the furloughing of felons like Horton was considered successful by corrections authorities. Obviously, questions like these were neither posed nor answered in the campaign spot. If they are going to be posed and answered, we must count upon a free media and the critical judgment of our fellow citizens to do so. And, indeed, the record shows that precisely this was done. In a nutshell, the point of the spot was that Dukakis' liberal views on criminal justice and incarceration were dangerous and had resulted in the Willie Horton incident which could have been prevented.

Critics argued that this campaign spot was especially offensive because it was racist. That Willie Horton was African-American, however, was not the point of the spot. In 1992, a sober recounting of the entire incident was presented in the British journal *The Economist*. This analysis did not find the ad to be racist, and reminded its readers that any citizen knowing what he or she believes in would hardly be impressed by the Willie Horton spot or any other negative ad.[1]

At the heart of the issue is our real problem with negative advertising, which is that we are convinced that other people are stupid and gullible. The salient question is not whether the Willie Horton spot offends the sensibilities of some of us. The question is whether placing contentious opinion before a mass audience must somehow constitute a corruption and debasement of public debate. Any political advertising spot is before the public to be judged, valued, and responded to like any the expression of any idea or opinion. And it is a fundamental index of liberty in a society that permits critics to voice their objections to the ad and to promote various interpretations of it. Are we fearful of negative political advertising or of our neighbors whom we consider dumb?

What was the effect of the Willie Horton spot on the 1988 election?

Precious little, I would guess, although how could anyone know for sure? Bush and Quayle likely won because they appeared as the successors to the Reagan presidency at a time when economic prosperity seemed adequate and the U.S.'s position in the world appeared to be satisfactory. Elections in the United States since the Second World War have been decided by such overarching perceptions in the electorate and not by TV spots or candidate images.

Political ads function like any other ads. They keep a candidate's name, or something identifiable about his or her positions, in front of the public. Much public discourse suggests that there is something undesirable or untoward about negative political advertising, yet what specifically is it? Especially in a political culture like the United State's in which ideological differences between politicians have tended to be blurred, in which there are many elected offices, and in which various referendums are voted upon, negative political advertising would appear to be a given. Saying in an ad that my opponent will vote to raise taxes, *a*) because he/she promotes the general idea of larger government with enhanced responsibilities, and/or *b*) because he/she supports specific programs that must be funded by tax revenues unless other spending cuts are made, is a perfectly plausible pitch for support. As a viewer, if I have decided that I oppose tax increases, then my knowing that candidate X holds a contrary view is perfectly good information. Conveying this information to me or to any other viewer in a negative TV ad is reasonable and ethical.

Let us say that I am a candidate for the U. S. Senate who supports abortion on demand. I produce a negative political ad presenting the information that, in 1988, as a member of the state legislature my opponent voted to limit public funding of abortions for women on welfare. Most viewers will be indifferent to the specifics of the ad. Some might reassess their support for me or for my opponent on the basis of it. Even those who do respond to my negative ad, however, will do so not because of the inherent power of the political spot itself. They will do so because this campaign spot focuses their attention on my opponent's record. If these voters support abortion on demand, it is not because they have arrived at that opinion based upon a thirty-second spot. Nor, by the way, will their position have much to do with whether they have seen a TV movie set in the bad old days in which a teenage character dies of complications of a botched back-alley abortion, or a contemporary TV episode in which a character goes through a legal abortion procedure and is back at her job the next day. Views on abortion are arrived at because of basic religious and philosophic points of view, our personal observations or experiences, our sense of fairness and compromise, our interpretation of constitutional protections and whether they apply more to an expectant mother's privacy or to an unborn baby's right to life, and our interpretation of what life is and when it begins.

Political ads are targeted at specific demographic groups and reinforce the basic axiom of electoral politics–to get out the vote. This assumes that nearly all voters know where they stand on the issues and how they are going to vote. The challenge, then, is to motivate them to get to the polls on election day. Political advertising spots are designed to mobilize and get out the vote that already exists in the population. Political advertising is not intended to produce major shifts in opinion. Rather, it is meant to keep certain candidates and issues in front of certain people. The strategy may backfire, of course, because tough negative campaigning might serve to mobilize voters for the opponent. The importance of political advertising is measurable almost entirely by the responsiveness of those who most likely can be encouraged to go to the polls on election day.

Negative advertising works to the extent that it is targeted precisely at those in the electorate who feel strongly enough on certain issues to translate their beliefs into actual votes. It is common for the Democratic Party's negative advertising to target Republican candidates who support tax cuts by implying that such cuts favor the wealthy at the cost of programs that are vital to many citizens. Republican advertising faults Democratic candidates for supporting permissiveness, failed social programs, and government policies that contribute to personal irresponsibility and waste or that infringe upon the rights of individuals. The Democrat's message of unfairness appeals especially to minorities, low income persons, and others who identify with the poor. The Republican message is aimed at middle and upper income groups, suburban and rural voters, as well as proponents of traditional values. Any individual may be motivated by what he or she does *not* want to see happen, which bespeaks only the complexity of contemporary issues and not the ethical bankruptcy of the citizenry. A portion of anyone's thought may be based upon the desire to avoid certain outcomes.

Critics maintain that TV's costs are hidden in the higher prices consumers pay for products and services that are advertised on it. There is a certain surface logic in this argument, of course. But in order for the quality and quantity of television production to be maintained at the levels that we have today, it is necessary for enormous investments in production to come from somewhere. The experience around the world is that public monies provided by government from tax revenues cannot provide sufficient funding for the sustained production of quality TV material. Advertising costs, moreover, do not necessarily impact you as an individual. I can enjoy a program sponsored by Revlon without ever buying a lipstick!

Since its inception, of course, television in the United States has existed to sell things. More precisely, television delivers audiences to advertisers who purchase commercial time based upon demographic projections of who will be watching. For many critics, such a structure appears to favor programming always aimed at the broadest mass audience. And that appearance surely adds fuel to the widespread assumption that TV programming is designed to appeal to only the "lowest common denominator." There are many nuances and subtleties within this generalization, however, and they are telling.

I recall a CBS executive who I met at a seminar sponsored by the American Film Institute to bring together academics who study the media with people from the industry. At one point in our conversation, he referred to some people as being more "demographically interesting" than others. The term, with which I was unfamiliar at the time, means that by age, income, and status some people are especially good prospects as consumers and others are not. Broadly speaking, the most demographically interesting people are twenty-five to fifty years old, well-educated, socially and geographically mobile, relatively affluent, reside in metropolitan areas, and have children living at home. People younger than twenty-five tend not to be well-established in their careers and incomes. People over fifty likely have gotten their children out-of-the home and are beginning to look and save seriously toward retirement.

People between the ages of twenty-five and fifty are the most consistently aggressive consumers. Both younger and older groups, of course, still engage in plenty of buying, but their spending is more specific. Those under twenty-five consume an inordinate proportion of the music cassettes and CDs sold, are big movie-goers, and eat lots of candy and fast food. Those over fifty (50) take more over-the-counter medications, go on more cruises, and might be interested in buying more insurance. Shifts in lifestyle affect these generalizations, but demographic projections still are relatively reliable.

Television's *Hee Haw*, for example, featuring country music and down-home humor, has always had large audiences in sheer numbers. But the people who are watching tend to be older, lower-income, and rural. Depending on your product, it generally is more advantageous to advertise on a program that appeals to a better educated and more upscale crowd. Still, there is scant evidence that the marketplace has not sufficed to provide viewers an abundant range of programming from which to choose. Now that satellite and cable systems are supplanting over-the-air broadcast everywhere, the *sole* curb upon variety and abundance in programming is governmental regulation and repression.

The best analysis of advertising is still the one published by William McGuire in the mid 1980s, in which he argued that although advertising was a $50-billion-a-year industry in the United States at the time, persistent or substantial advertising effects could not be demonstrated conclusively. McGuire's contention was followed, several years later, by the findings of Gerard Tellis at the University of Iowa who maintained unequivocally that the claimed effects of television advertising on consumers could not be demonstrated.[2] Indeed, television viewers should all thank the heavens for the fact that advertisers continue to buy TV time in spite of considerable evidence that such advertising is not effective. If they didn't, the production values seen in television programming all around the world would plummet dramatically.

By now, the notion that the masses are victims of the media is firmly embedded in contemporary culture. Such a view has its roots not only in the wellsprings of our specific discontents with television, but also in the general drift that thought and culture have taken since the 1960s. The sophisticated sources of this idea of victimization can be traced back to the "Frankfurt School" of social thought that gave so much credence to the supposed link between media manipulation and the rise of Hitler and the Nazis. The more general source is the perception that those individuals and groups who are less successful than others are, inevitably, in some way "victimized." Such thinking is widely prevalent, and is also at the heart of complaints and criticism about advertising. For example, Leslie Savan who writes for *The Village Voice* argues that it is our "advertising culture" that makes people restless and unhappy. Savan's premise is highly problematic, but still I find value in the fact that she points out that if all the logos, labels, and announcements are counted, then the average American sees roughly 16,000 ads every day![3] Rather than being glum and pessimistic about this fact, however, I would point out that it must mean that in nearly all of those 16,000 instances people are looking right through or beyond the message being sent their way. There can be no other conclusion than that individuals are selective and critical, exercise their reason and use their judgment, and that each of us responds to ads on the basis of perceived self-interest.

NOTES

1. *The Economist*, January 25, 1992.

2. William J. McGuire, "The Myth of Massive Media Impact: Savagings and Salvagings," in George Comstock, ed., *Public Communication and Behavior* (Orlando: Academic Press, 1986), pp. 173-257. See also, Nina Lentini, "Stop Wasting Money Researcher Tells TV Advertisers," *Adweek*, April 17, 1989, pp. 40, 41.

3. Quoted in John Garvey, "Commercials," *Commonweal*, February 10, 1995.

8

Television and Government

Many interpreters of contemporary culture see the public as fickle and undiscriminating. Yet what is the evidence that people are not making judgments on the basis of strongly held beliefs and values, critical thinking, and a sifting through of the data as it becomes available to them? Individuals in mass society continually discriminate in all kinds of matters, both significant and petty. Who really believes that citizens at the end of the twentieth century are less critical and discerning than they were fifty, or a hundred, or even two hundred years ago? We may not agree with the latest election results or like the list of the top ten TV shows as based on the ratings, but we cannot deny that individuals are making specific choices in both instances.

There is a difference between rigorous thinking about society and culture that is based upon the assembling and working through of data, as opposed to a science of society and culture. We may measure intelligence fairly well, insofar as IQ-tests give us good statistics for predicting success in school and academic cognitive ability. But we cannot test for sensitivity, or taste, or judgment. We can obtain precise statistics for the number of divorces in a given year in the United States, but we recognize that each divorce in that year has its specific causes and its own uniqueness.

We can learn much from laboratory experiments with animals that carry over to humans, such as the effects of certain drugs on the organism, the causal relationships of certain substances to illness or its cure, and even the likely causes of helplessness or depression. But we cannot use laboratory animals to demonstrate the effects of watching daily episodes of *Beavis and Butt-head*, just as we cannot extrapolate from another species what someone may be thinking after watching an episode of *Murphy Brown* or *60 Minutes*.

Even substances known to affect the human body do so in very different ways. Take, for example, alcohol and animal fats. If a human ingests drinkable alcohol, after some amount is consumed, he or she will enter a state of intoxication. The amount consumed before this condition is reached may vary considerably and is influenced by several factors: body weight; whether one has eaten or not; whether one is accustomed to drinking alcohol; genetic structure; one's metabolism and body chemistry. Nonetheless, a highly demonstrable hypothesis still holds: When humans ingest drinkable alcohol in sufficient amounts, dependent upon several variables, they become intoxicated. If we take one hundred subjects and cause each of them to consume alcohol in quantities that we have determined sufficient to intoxicate the normal subject, then we expect most of our subjects to become drunk. As each one becomes intoxicated, we anticipate observing generalized reactions. The drunken subjects all will lose some degree of physical coordination, the speed and precision of their responses to stimuli will decrease, their speech will become slurred, and their functions of perception and motor response will be impaired. On the other hand, certain responses will vary greatly and may contradict one another. Some of our drunks will become talkative and happy, while others may become sullen and morose. Some will want to party, calling to the experimenters to bring on the hats and horns. Others will want to go off alone to sulk in their tents.

In the case of ingesting animal fats, unlike our short-term test with alcohol, we cannot structure a similar experiment. If we wish to test the hypothesis that the ingestion of animal fats produces elevated cholesterol levels in humans, and that these elevated cholesterol levels increase the likelihood of coronary disease, we do not assemble a hundred subjects, sit them all down at a table, and cause each of them to eat a 24-ounce sirloin or a pound of fried bacon. Even if we did, we would not expect to learn anything about the relationship of serum blood cholesterol levels to heart disease. We might expect nearly all our subjects to feel uncomfortably full, with some of them becoming physically ill. We would predict nothing further, however. In the case of studying the interrelationships of animal fats, cholesterol, and heart disease, we would expect to reach viable conclusions only after protracted, longitudinal studies over time.

And, even then, our conclusions would be more tentative and our claim of causal relationships less conclusive than in the case of the alcohol study.

Tests meant to assess media influence on individuals, both in the past and at present, are conducted as if what was being studied were short-term effects. I know of no studies that demonstrate the direct effects of specific media presentations on individual behavior over time. And we have really never needed a research apparatus to demonstrate such impacts. Moreover, the filters and resistance of TV viewers to what they see and hear are growing, not declining. Television audiences on the eve of the twenty-first century are critical and skeptical, and they have lots of choices. Nowhere in the world is there demonstrably less information or fewer choices for entertainment than there were fifty years ago. The close of the 1980s brought not only the collapse of communism in Eastern Europe and a quantum leap in the free exchange of ideas, images, and stories, but also the proliferation of a variety of communications technologies, including satellite and cable television and the Internet. There is more of every form of contemporary art, information, entertainment, or amalgamation thereof than ever before, and this trend continues. There will be more TV channels in the future, not fewer. There will be more videotapes and a greater variety of outlets for their dissemination. There will be more movies and more ways of watching them in more different places. But clearly this global cultural democratization has outstripped its political counterpart. Governments everywhere are still basing policies toward the media arts upon theories of their negative effects both on individuals and on society at large. On just such grounds, ostensibly, governments remain unyieldingly committed to regulating television.

It is interesting to wonder whether a Hitler or a Stalin would have been less likely to triumph and dominate in the age of television than, in fact, they each did right on the eve of its advent. Had camera crews been following General Sherman's march through Georgia in the American Civil War or had there been nightly news coverage of Confederate mothers and their children suffering during the siege of Vicksburg, would these pictures have eroded the popular will of citizens in the North to continue the war? And had that happened, might not the institution of slavery have survived in the South?

It is easier to gain access to the media today, but also more difficult to hide corruption, repression, and atrocity. And while frequently we are troubled by the fact that the fictions filling the screens of our movie theaters and televisions sets do not match up to the best of their written predecessors in storytelling, the fact is that today more people everywhere in the world have more access to a variety of vicarious pleasure than ever before. More does not necessarily mean better, but neither does it mean the opposite. As this abundance of art and entertainment grows, and as new technologies spread to distant corners of the globe, two things become increasingly necessary with regard to the position that we take as citizens toward the media and public policy:

1. The increasing number of stories, images, and information in our world
    require increasing energy on the part of individuals to select and discrimi-
    nate among them.
2. That governments be put under increasing pressure to adhere to a hands-off
    policy with regard to images, ideas, and stories and the free exchange of
    them around the globe.

In the United States, First Amendment protections that apply to print never have been extended to television. Like radio, TV is continually subject to governmental control through the Federal Communications Commission (FCC). If someone went on TV or radio and simply read passages from many controversial books found in nearly any public library, the broadcaster could be threatened with heavy fines or the possible loss of a license.

This federal regulatory body has never confined itself to technical matters such as preventing one broadcast signal from interfering with another. Instead, the FCC controls the ownership and licensing of stations and networks, monitors program content and language, restricts the type of material transmitted and at what time of day it may air, regulates advertising, and even mandates that stations provide certain kinds of programming.

While the incessant Puritanism of the Motion Picture Production Code is only a historic memory in Hollywood today,[1] the FCC still bans references to or depictions of certain situations on TV. During Ronald Reagan's years in the White House, the Federal Communications Commission took several limited steps toward deregulating broadcasting. Commercial speech was granted increased protection and the Fairness Doctrine that required broadcasters to balance informational program-ming was suspended. A more open approach to broadcast and cable television licensing was taken by the FCC during those years. There was, however, an immediate retreat from these positions after George Bush entered the White House, and a wholesale reversal of policy after President Bill Clinton took office in January, 1993. The FCC's membership consists of political appointees and so its directions shift with the political winds.

During the 1990s the Federal Communications Commission has become a focal point for pressure on broadcasters. One attempt to use the FCC in a brazen political manner has consisted of congressional efforts to make the FCC restore the Fairness Doctrine. This initiative became known in the halls on Capitol Hill as the "Hush-Rush" movement, its intent being to make it far more difficult for opinionated commentators like Rush Limbaugh to keep their radio and TV shows on the air. Under a restored Fairness Doctrine, zealously enforced by the FCC, a station broadcasting Limbaugh's show could be required to provide equal time for those who might disagree with his views. Congressional Democrats and others see in the Fairness Doctrine a mechanism to force stations broadcasting opinionated political views to balance such programs by offering free air time to opponents.[2] But this effort at restoring the Fairness Doctrine, which peaked right before Republicans gained control of Congress in the 1994 elections, has proven to be quite unnecessary. Alas, even the fate of opinionated commentators like Limbaugh rises and falls according to audience response.[3]

Government control over media content looks and feels acceptable to most of us. But we need to step back and ask ourselves why. Just where will our scapegoating of television and our denial of First Amendment protection to the media arts and broadcasting take us? The president of the United States, Bill Clinton, heralded legislation requiring V chips in TV sets and a rating system for television programs in the 1996 Telecommunications Act. On close examination, however, most of us would be appalled at just how complicated, expensive, and capricious its enforcement is likely to be. Scratch its facade and like all such legislation pertaining to TV broadcast and cable material, this law runs smack into the problem of slippery definitions. Regulators from the federal government finally must decide just what is considered permissible and what is held to cross the line. The language of their guidelines points toward a morass of slippery and arbitrary judgments. The result likely will be lawsuits galore and a staggering repression of free speech along the way.

What, for example, is "worthwhile" children's programming on TV? Just that term was used in a 1990 federal law that the FCC has been enforcing ever since.[4] Better yet, just what is "violence?" It has become the mother of all buzzwords when it comes to talking about politics and television at the end of the 1990s. What, however, is a definition of violence upon which we can agree? Is violence one spaceship zapping another? Photos of Nicole Brown Simpson's bruised face shown by the prosecution and seen on Court-TV or CNN? A woman's slap to the face of a masher/harasser in a drama set in the workplace? A boxing match? What about that 1940s cartoon I remember from my childhood of those mice tying dynamite sticks to kitty's behind and blasting him to kingdom come? Or Ralph Cramdon's inevitable line delivered in every episode of that 1950s TV classic *The Honeymooners*: "One of these days Alice, pow, right in the kisser!"? Sure smacks of spousal abuse to me. Will the federally mandated rating system warn and protect our children from reruns of *The Honeymooners*? Well, we all better hope so or else the 1996 telecommunications law will not be doing nearly enough to prevent domestic violence, will it? Federal lawmakers assure us that news will be exempted from the violence labels and they have written that language into the law. But what precisely is meant by "news?" A nightly newscast to be sure, but what about an episode of *Hard Copy*, *Rivera Live*, *60 Minutes*, or *Cochran and Company* on Court-TV?[5]

The powers of the FCC are great and the position of its mandates under the law appear to be solid. In 1995, the commission's ban on the telecasting of "indecent" programming between 6:00 in the morning and midnight was upheld by the Supreme Court of the United States.[6] Radio "shock jock" Howard Stern has cost his employers hundreds of thousands of dollars in fines levied by the FCC for a few naughty words and an off-color joke.[7] During the 1990s, the FCC has become increasingly menacing toward broadcasters with similar threats of fines or the revoking of station licenses.

Alongside the powers of the FCC, the introduction of new manda-tory technologies promises individual families further control over what enters their homes on the TV set. Apparently a substantial number of Americans believe that it must be good to enable parents to control what their children might be able to see on television. Congressional support for a government mandate that V chips *must* be installed in *all* TV sets sold in the United States was overwhelming. The idea that parents should be able to more effectively control what is coming into their homes sounds reasonable enough, but there are three problems with the provisions that were written into the 1996 Telecommunications Act.

The first is philosophic and goes to the heart of judging what is the appropriate role of government. The V chip mandate increases the cost of buying a TV set for everyone, even though the requirement has nothing to do with public health or safety. And to what end? Surely, the marketplace can function adequately to sell TV sets with V chips or similar blocking devices to those customers who have an interest in buying them. Why make it mandatory for every new set sold in America to be equipped with this device?

The second problem is a practical one having to do with the device itself. If the V chip system is easy enough for "any parent in America" to program it, just how long do we think it will take the average eleven-year-old to figure out how to do a little reverse programming to be able to consume the forbidden television fruit? Some researchers have already concluded that the V chip and the rating system most probably will tempt a number of youngsters to try to tune into programming that they otherwise would never have thought of watching.[8] Forbidden fruit probably looks more tasty, especially to the young and the restless.

The third problem is a legal matter. Producers will have to rate and label their programming. But are such ratings easily agreed upon? Government regulators, and subsequently the courts, still will have to decide whenever there are disagreements over a program's content rating. If you like federal bureaucracy and regulatory nightmares, or it you have an abiding passion for litigation and court battles, then this government-mandated rating system for TV programming is certain to be a bonanza. One major network already has indicated that it will resist the ratings altogether.

The V chip blocking system fits hand in glove with a rating system The latter has worked well enough with the movies, or so most people think. But the rating system for the movies is an entirely *voluntary* one controlled solely by the Motion Picture Association of America, a private trade organization consisting of the major corporations that produce and distribute movies shown in theaters throughout the United States. These movie ratings are neither monitored, nor sponsored, nor controlled by the government. The ratings of G, PG, PG-13, R, and NC-17 are self-assessments endorsed by the movie makers and theater owners who participate in this system, and they have no status in law. Moreover, the movie ratings apply only to feature films produced or distributed for theatrical release by the major companies that are MPAA members. This totals some 400-to-600 hours of film a year. By contrast, just a *single* TV station that is on for 24-hours-a-day presents *9,000 hours* of programming each year.[9] The sheer volume of the programming to be dealt with, and the problematic nature of terms like worthwhile, indecent, violence, and news boggles the mind.

How did American society reach the point at which such benighted and repressive legislation could sail through Congress? There are a number of political and cultural ways to explain this, but an overarching reason is the respectability given to such legislation by media effects researchers. At a cost of over three million dollars researchers at the University of California, Santa Barbara, the University of Texas at Austin, the University of North Carolina at Chapel Hill, and the University of Wisconsin at Madison, for example, have teamed up to produce yet a new analysis of the state of violence on American television for the late 1990s.[10] This ambitious monitoring program is based upon the assumption that "the context of a violent act or portrayal is crucial," and upon a definition of violence as any "use of physical force, or credible threat of physical force."[11]

Content analysis of television programming is continually used to support claims that what is on television and what is going on in America are directly linked. There is a built-in assumption underlying all the media effects research that holds that media exposure will create behavior. Surely, these claims vary, from a somewhat dated and simplistic imitation theory to the seemingly more sophisticated cultivation theory that is now in vogue. But no matter what the nuances, the end result is claimed to be the same:

1. Viewers will learn aggressive attitudes and behavior.
2. Viewers will become desensitized to real violence.
3. Viewers will exhibit the "fear effect" and mistrust others.[12]

Indeed, the research apparatus, and the public's attention to such findings, likely reached a high point in the mid 1990s, even as violent crime rates began decreasing all across America. Actually, the researchers in mass communication tend to exhibit cavalier attitudes toward the ebbs and flows of the crime statistics. In fact, crime rates go up and down, contingent upon a number of variables–the primary one being the number of fifteen to twenty-five year old males in the population–but there is no direct correlation between what is on TV and the number of crimes. Crime rose in the United States in the late 1980s and early 1990s. It had begun to decrease nearly everywhere in the country by 1995, and was plummeting dramatically after that. That the "effects" research does not match up precisely to crime statistics is one kind of error in its design, but more importantly this body of inquiry precedes on the basis of a fundamental and pervasive error in its concept. As W. Russell Neuman of the Annenberg School of Communication at the University of Pennsylvania points out: "There is no evidence of consistent or significant differences in the abilities of different media to persuade, inform, or even instill emotional response in audience members."[13] You may be moved and impressed by all sorts of media and all sorts of messages: a sermon at church, a sunset you saw on the coast of France, something you read, a lecture you heard, a song on the radio or one that you heard someone whistling while walking in the park. The notion that television has some sort of diabolical control over–and effect upon–its viewers *could* easily be dismissed as wild and arcane were it not so widely believed.

And, indeed, it *is* widely believed, and that belief is being constantly fueled by one sort of claim or another. Alas, the apparatus of the "effects" researchers and their well-oiled machinery lurches forward under its own truly myopic dynamic offering the same old bromides that have persisted for decades. There are different sorts of studies, with different sources of funding, and they exhibit different spins upon how the data that they generate is to be interpreted. Since 1995, the Center for Communications Policy at the University of California at Los Angeles, for example, has been conducting surveys of violence on television under the sponsorship of the four major commercial networks in the United States (ABC, CBS, Fox, and NBC). These studies at UCLA are sometimes maintained to differ from other research efforts because instead of simply counting violent acts they also interpret each depiction contextually.[14] Nonetheless, the context referred to by these researchers is solely one defined by the particular dramatic action that occurs in a program. No one is talking about the context of reception which is the point at which an individual perceives the show from the position of his or her distinct point of view.

Definitely not all of these researchers agree on solutions to the *problem* of violence on TV, which, it must be noted, is a problem that they have concocted. The director of the study at UCLA, Jeffrey Cole, appears to be counting on the networks to decrease the amount of violence in network programming.[15] Ellen Wartella, a prominent figure in this field from the University of Texas, for example, is no supporter of the V chip which she dismisses as a "technological fix" that will not arm parents sufficiently to navigate the turbulent waters of TV-violence on their children's behalf.[16] Yet coming from such researchers, arguments against the V chip appear to me to be disingenuous. They may personally believe in other solutions, but it is precisely the on going efforts of the mass communication research establishment since the 1960s that have convinced pundits, politicians, and the public that the threats to society from violence on television are real. The result of accepting that general contention can *only* be some sort of fix.

While Wartella argues for more media education rather than for the V chip, the critic Malcolm Gladwell writing in *The New Yorker* promotes yet a different objection to the chip. His complaint is that the technology will work well enough and that the V chip is a satisfactory device insofar as it will be used. Federal law, however, requires only that the V chip be mandatory in *new* television sets, which he points out means that V chips will *not* become available to those parents who he thinks need them the most. Those families, according to Gladwell, are "lower income, ill-educated" and the least able to afford a new television set.[17]

Gladwell gives his readers a strikingly undisguised insight into a significant social and cultural dynamic behind many of the calls for control over television programming. As two sage commentators, Martin Barker and Julian Petley, have observed throughout their edited volume of essays entitled *Ill Effects: The Media/Violence Debate* (1997), contemporary concerns about the suspected pernicious effects of sex and violence on TV stand right in line with what they call "the history of respectable fears" dating back to the mid-nineteenth century. At the heart of the matter is an unrelenting demand in society for control over the entertainments and diversions of the "dangerous classes." With regard to television, governments try to control and prohibit certain programming on behalf of the "educated" and the "cultured" in society who hope this will prevent the lower social orders from running amok. As part of this effort, a well-funded research apparatus has proven all too willing to provide the so-called "scientific" argument to justify these efforts.[18]

In the worldwide debate over liberty and democracy during the last quarter of the twentieth century, broadcasting has not received nearly the attention that it deserves. Even in the most free societies there exists a social contract that treats broadcasting by broad consensus as a special case. True enough, in Western Europe broadcasting was opened to private ownership and competition during the 1980s.[19] In the United States, some limitations on ownership of stations and some broadcast and cablecast practices were loosened. Yet nowhere is true deregulation of broadcasting, cable, and satellite being actively promoted, and nowhere are the airwaves truly free. A 1992 study by UNESCO found television not only to still be controlled directly by the government in 102 countries, but also concluded that "even in the most democratic countries, political authorities have never entirely relinquished their influence over the television industry."[20] Worldwide, media freedom remains an entirely elusive and unfulfilled idea. Restrictions prevail both in the United States and abroad, and furthermore, cries for additional limitations on program content and broadcasters' rights are in vogue on the eve of the twenty-first century.

NOTES

1. See, Raymond Moley, *The Hays Office* (New York: Bobbs-Merrill, 1945) and Gerald Gardiner, *The Censorship Papers: Movie Censorship Letters from the Hays Office, 1934-1968* (New York: Dodd, Mead, 1987).

2. John Corry, "Fairness Most Foul," *The American Spectator*, November, 1995, pp. 50, 51.

3. Neil Gabler, "Endangered Species," *George Magazine*, May, 1997.

4. Richard Zoglin, "If Not the Jetsons, What?" *Time*, March 22, 1993, p. 64.

5. Nick Gillespie, "Chip Off the Block," *Reason*, November, 1995, p. 7.

6. Edward L. Andrews, "Court Upholds Ban on Indecent Broadcasting Programming," *The New York Times*, July 1, 1995, p. 7. A lower court had struck down the FCC's ban on these, broadcasts during the day and evening as an infringement to the rights of adults to view such materials, as reported in *The New York Times*, November 24, 1993, p. A1.

7. Bill Carter, "Stern Reportedly Rules Out Late-Night Talk Show," *The New York Times*, January 5, 1994, C22.

8. "Report: TV Ratings May Lure Youngsters to Racy Shows," *Showbiz Story Page*, March 26, 1997.

9. Gillespie, *Chip*, p. 7.

10. See the *National Television Violence Study, Executive Summary*, Vol. 1 (March, 1996) and Volume 2 (March, 1997), Santa Barbara, CA: The Center for Communication and Social Policy.

11. Ellen A. Wartella, *The Context of Television Violence* (Needham Heights, MA: Allen and Bacon, 1997), pp. 2, 3.

12. ibid., p. 6.

13. W. Russell Neuman, *The Future of the Mass Audience* (Cambridge: Cambridge University Press, 1991), p. 99.

14. Brian Lowry, "Study Finds Improvement in Handling On-Air Violence," *Los Angeles Times*, January 14, 1998.

15. ibid.

16. Wartella, *Context*, pp. 9, 10.

17. Malcom Gladwell, "Cheap Thrills: There's More to TV Than V. There's Also T.," *The New Yorker*, April 19, 1997.

18. Martin Baker and Julian Petley, "Introduction," *Ill Effects: The Media/Violence Debate*, edited by Baker and Petley (New York/London: Routledge, 1997), p. 5.

19. Hevre Michel and Anne-Laure Angoulvent, *Les Télévisions en Europe* (Paris: Presses Universitaire de France, 1992).

20. Jean-Claude Guilleband, "A Mysterious Medium," *Unesco Courier*, October, 1992.

9

Art for Whose Sake?

Direct government ownership of the electronic media has been common-place in most of the world historically. In some countries, with the United States as the prime example, television has been privately owned but nonetheless regulated by the government. The question of the extent of governmental ownership and regulation would appear to be the primary issue in public policy toward television. And that it is, on the surface. The deeper questions underlying public policy toward television are: What is art? and What should be the government's relationship to art in a democracy? I must conclude that these two questions continue to be answered, across the breadth of society in nations all around the world, without regard to the enormous changes in art during the twentieth century.

Since shortly after World War II these changes have accelerated exponentially and expanded globally. Nonetheless, most cultural debate continues to frame questions regarding the relationship of government to art as if these changes had never occurred. In nearly all quarters there prevails the assumption that the nature of art remains immutable and that the pre-democratic patronage of art by rulers and elites is a legacy that must be carried on in contemporary democracies by governmental agencies. This notion of supporting art through public funding, more-over, conforms neatly with the idea of governmental control over television, either by direct ownership or by regulation.

The historical patronage of the arts by ecclesiastical, royal, and aristocratic entities in Europe, however, could never be effectively and justifiably transferred to the sovereignty of the modern democratic state. Nonetheless, since the Second World War, just this dogma has prevailed in those modern states where it is considered the responsibility of government to be directly responsible for the general welfare of the citizenry. This idea was first fostered in its contemporary guise in Western Europe. Subsequently, it was absorbed into public policy in the United States when Congress established the NEA (National Endowment for the Arts) and CPB (the Corporation for Public Broadcasting, which funds public television and radio) in the late 1960s. Their creation meshed with the already well established control over radio and television by government through the Federal Communications Commission and legislation dating back to 1934.

For two decades, the NEA and the CPB lumbered along with no serious challenge to them and with scant public debate about their appropriateness. Then in 1989 several members of the United States' Congress drew attention to decisions by the National Endowment for the Arts that had permitted grants to partially support the production or exhibition of works that they found offensive. One of these was *The Piss Christ*, a creative inspiration of Andrés Serrano. It is a photograph of a small plastic crucifix submerged in a bottle of yellow liquid that the artist described as his own urine. By titling the work as he did, it may be assumed that part of the artist's intention was to affront the sensibilities of believing Christians who have faith that Jesus is divine. A substantial number of Christians, no doubt, regarded Serrano's work as a silly and infantile display unworthy of their further concern. Some may even have considered it to be a good example of photographic art because of its technical qualities, remaining content to assess its meaning and value solely on that basis. There was even room, of course, to interpret *The Piss Christ* as simply drawing attention to the way in which Jesus is represented pictorially and, hence, not being necessarily anti-religious. Others, however, found the work to be offensive, derogatory, and inflammatory, and objected specifically to having the production or exhibition of such art subsidized by their tax monies.

In assessing the fundamental issues posed by this incident, as well as general questions pertaining to public funding for the arts, two principles apply:

1. Government has no inherent nor legitimate interest in preventing any citizen from viewing "The Piss Christ" or any other work of art. We may consider

a work to be offensive, but it is not the role of the state either to control or limit its exhibition.

2. The corollary to premise # 1 is that government has no inherent nor legitimate interest in providing for the production or exhibition of *The Piss Christ*. The state has no reason to provide a subsidy to a work of art, to favor any specific art form with a subsidy, or to underwrite the production or exhibition of art generally.

Protests about *The Piss Christ* and several other performances or exhibitions funded by the NEA generated a subsequent protracted public debate that, in essence, focused upon the wrong issues. Many critics of the NEA appeared to be claiming that works created or exhibited with public monies do not have First Amendment protection. Such a position, however, is untenable, for protections of speech and expression apply equally to any work whether it is sanctioned by government subsidy or not. On the other hand, the defenders of the NEA appeared to take the position that it did not matter if public funds were used to assault the deepest beliefs of a particular group of citizens. This position is equally untenable. Any governmental agency might be expected at least to apologize for its part in abetting a work of art aimed at being so hurtful. Indeed, had Serrano submerged a plastic Star of David in yellow liquid with a photograph of a victim of the Nazi death camps and titled it *The Piss Jew*, then in many jurisdictions in the United States, instead of receiving public funds to subsidize the work's dissemination, he would have been prosecuted for a hate crime.

Grants from government coffers for art that is as silly and as offensive as *The Piss Christ* have been rare. Most of the spending by the NEA and the various states arts councils goes to established organizations, such as the Metropolitan Opera Company in New York City, which consistently has been the NEA's largest beneficiary for a number of years. Such organizations do not use their grants for works that are controversial, but the basic question is why should tax monies be spent to support any particular art form at all?

One argument for such spending is pragmatic. Governmental spending for the arts has an economic impact that goes beyond the artists and arts administrators supported directly by such funds. As a carful of wealthy ladies motor into Manhattan from the suburbs for a night at the opera, they buy gasoline. Behind the bullet-proof glass at the station where they fill up, the young woman cashier benefits. The NEA's subsidy to the Metropolitan Opera, where the average ticket costs in the seventy to eighty dollar range, has an economic ripple effect.

The argument, however, that such public spending on the arts contributes significantly and necessarily to economic development is far-fetched, circular, and peripheral. Government spending on anything distributes money into society, of course, but public monies had to come out of society first in the form of taxes. There are many governmental schemes for redistributing wealth, nearly all of which are highly suspect. But, even among government's most questionable programs and economic policies, given the demographics of the audiences for opera in the United States this particular subsidy must be labeled as being both regressive and unnecessary.

Certain individuals do benefit directly from governmental subsidies to the arts, of course–namely selected artists and their audiences. As a special interest lobby they provide effective pressure on Congress and the various state legislatures for such funding. But this particular lobbying assiduously disguises its narrow and self-interested intentions by aiming its arguments at what are claimed to be the better instincts of lawmakers.

The entire debate over the NEA and public funding for the arts is as heated as it is, and draws attention that is grossly disproportionate to the amount of funding involved, because it constitutes a debate over what art and culture are. Support for the arts is justified as spending public tax dollars because of a belief that can be expressed in this equation: Good art contributes to the goodness of people who, in turn, produce goodness in society. This received idea is widespread and relatively uncontested, even among people who have never given any other serious thought to art and its nature. Some version of this premise pervades both the educational system and the media, as well as lurking just below the surface in nearly all casual conversation on the matter.

From the origins of the species, humans danced, sang, beat sticks together, or blew air through reeds. They made masks, put on make up, and joined in performances known as rituals. They gathered, told, and listened to stories. They molded figures in clay and carved them from stone. They drew or painted upon the walls of their caves. Humans did all these things, in fact, before they did nearly anything else. Art came before the domestication of animals and agriculture, the building of roads, the origins of science, and the founding of either engineering or medicine. A fundamental impulse to art is basic to humans. That impulse, however, is a far cry from a soprano's embellishments on the stage of the Metropolitan Opera or Michael Jackson's grabbing his crotch in a music video on MTV!

It is only from the origins of man to the present, and with regard to the fundamental nature of art and its subsequent permutations and transformations over time, that television's place in society and culture can be understood. Art was originally central to the belief systems of tribal and communal groups. Only in the twentieth century has art become commonplace and access to it widespread, which means that art is also becoming coincidental. Art has traced its path from origins among clans and kin, through centuries of patronage by the church, royalty, aristocracy, and the wealthy, to today's competitive market system. Art has gone from being tribal, through being the province of specific classes and nations, to being global. In contemporary circumstances, art consists of various decorations and entertainments appealing to different tastes.

The aesthetic of repetition, now based in large part upon the electronic technologies developed during the twentieth century, celebrates the ascendancy of audience taste. Hence, "taste" is the central issue in contemporary cultural criticism, although almost no one studies or discusses it seriously.[1] The traditionalist position is that taste is a matter of veneration and appreciation to be passed on from one generation to the next. Education not only cultivates our respect for a canon of selected works, but also provides us the means to shape our taste for the arts in the present. Good taste, then, means favoring those arts in direct proportion to their capacity to meet the expectations of a traditional western aesthetic of virtuosity. By contrast, a radical position posits that popular taste is a manifestation of "false consciousness." Education, then, should point toward a new consciousness resulting in tastes aligned with the authentic class interests of the masses in challenging the economic, social, and cultural interests of elites. Hence, people should be interested in art in direct proportion to its capacity to undermine the assumptions and power upon which the ruling social order is based. Both these views are severely limited and deeply flawed.

For 2,500 years democratic theory has promised much. Finally, at the end of the twentieth century, it has begun to deliver on its promises in ways infinitely more profound than ever before. Good taste and refinement, however, are not among those promises. The notion that such qualities translate into forms of goodness and worth benefitting the whole of society, moreover, is hardly even ancient wisdom. Plato, after all, concluded that poets had no worthwhile place in the republic and argued that they should be banished from it. It is untenable to maintain that people who choose what they wish are not getting what they need in terms of entertainment and decoration.

Early in the nineteenth century, at the dawn of the industrial age, the Scottish philosopher Jeremy Bentham observed that with regard to its social usefulness, push-pins, which was a kind of bowling game, was as good as poetry.[2] This sage observation points us toward recognizing that there is no corollary between good art and good behavior, social order, or civic virtue. In Italy, extraordinarily accomplished visual art was produced for centuries. In those very same centuries, however, conditions of life along the Italian peninsula could hardly have been said to have been beneficent for most of the population. The Medici family in Florence may have commissioned some of the world's greatest painting and sculpture. They hardly were interested, however, in enlightening their own rule by their exposure to it. For all its grand painting and sculpture, along with its rich theatrical traditions such as the *commedia del arte*, and its definitive elaborations of grand opera, Italy's social, economic, and political life was plagued for centuries. Feudalism held on doggedly alongside dreadfully inefficient public institutions, and blended all too easily into fascism early in the twentieth century. Italy emerged from this legacy of backwardness only after the Second World War. Neighboring Switzerland, by contrast, which has contributed far less to the artistic heritage of the West, has been a stable and prosperous society, with strong representative institutions, for the better part of a thousand years.

What is true of nations is also true for individuals. Biographies of some of the most accomplished artists reveal lives of hard work, kindness, devotion, and principle. Others, just as prominent, have tawdry records. The same holds for followers of the arts. Elevated taste never ensures good judgment and moral integrity. More than one Nazi death camp commandant who butchered innocents by day spent his evenings listening to the recorded music of Bach, Beethoven, and Brahms.

If there is no direct corollary between art and behavior, then why promote public policies that use taxpayer monies to subsidize the production and/or exhibition of certain works of art on the one hand, while government controls repress the free exchange of ideas and images through the media arts on the other? Art is not life. The sculptor Alberto

Giacometti phrased the heart of the matter in the following rhetorical question that he posed to help us understand art's true nature. Imagine, he argued, that a building were on fire and that inside it were a painting and a cat. If that painting was a priceless masterpiece and the feline an ordinary alley cat, and you could save only one, which would you choose? Giacometti's unflinching answer was that he would save the cat.

If we bandy about false claims about art and its nature, we do not only a disservice to truth but also to art itself. The United States today is awash in art, as are many societies around the globe. Music fills the air and the airwaves. The last radio/audiocassette player that I purchased was a Walkman-type that I got at a discount store for nine dollars. It delivers stations playing classical, rock, country, reggae, jazz, and mood music. It plays any audio cassette that I choose to hear. Turn on the television as you pass by the set in your living room and out comes drama and comedy galore. Glance at a copy of *The National Geographic* on the coffee table with an exquisite landscape photo on its cover. One credible estimate calculates the amount being spent annually on art and entertainment in the United States in the mid-1990s at $340 billion,[3] and this includes a lot of "fine art." Sheldon Hackney, while Chairman of the National Endowment for the Humanities, the sister agency to the NEA, boasted that New York City's Metropolitan Museum of Art was attracting more paid attendance each year than *all* the sports events in the city put together![4] The critic Robert Hughes has estimated that more Americans go to art museums each year than go to all the football games played at all levels nationwide.[5] But then why do the arts demand largesse from the coffers of government? Maybe there should be a program of federal grants for the likes of the New York Knickerbockers professional basketball team, or the rail huggers at Aqueduct Race Track, or the New York Yankees.

But then, of course, sporadic government handouts to wealthy sports franchises do exist. Indiana University professor Mark S. Rosentraub's 1997 book, *Major League Losers: The Real Costs of Sports and Who's Paying for It*, goes a long way toward exposing the nonsense of such subsidies. His research provides excellent data to effectively refute the imagined relationship between sports, economic development, and civic pride that is relied upon by governmental bodies to justify pouring taxpayer dollars into the support of wealthy professional sports franchises.[6]

What exactly is government trying to support and for whom? Many of us feel that we have an abiding attachment to live music. But is that to be explained solely in terms of our artistic pleasure? Most of us can enjoy music with better sound and with more personal comfort at home than in a concert hall. If you are a sensualist who wants to wallow in sound you can invest in a pair of great speakers, crank up the volume, remove all your clothes, and settle naked into your plushiest chair after pouring yourself a glass of the best wine that you can afford.

As an aesthetic issue, it may be important to recognize the particular powers of presence in a live performance, to assess and discuss those qualities critically, and to encourage people to give due consideration to attending live musical performances and theatre events. It constitutes both flawed aesthetic education and erroneous public policy, however, to support artistic and cultural forms simply because they are traditional but confront growing costs and/or eroding audience support. Yet, precisely the notion that society should preserve dying art forms and venues is alive and well in the government's official arts bureaucracy. Just such thinking must have been called upon to justify the three grants awarded by the National Endowment of The Arts to the financially troubled side-shows at Coney Island in the mid-1990s.[7] Providing public funding for the continuing exhibition of the Bearded Lady or the Three Legged Woman is an exceptional instance of a stab at preservation that makes no sense at all, but other efforts to save art forms that cannot survive on their own are just as benighted. Change is an inherent condition of culture, and artists and the arts are challenged to undergo adaptation to change just like other people and other activities.

The truths about culture and cultural change are complex, as is the entire question of which art forms survive and why. Neither television and radio, nor videocassettes and sound recordings, have destroyed the audience for live performances or movie theaters, although they may have taken a toll on audience numbers in certain places and for certain types of presentations. In the near future we will be able to dial the phone, order nearly any movie of our choice to be transmitted into our home, and watch it on a fairly large screen with high definition visuals and digital sound. Movie theaters still will be around, however, so long as people want to get out of the house once in awhile, go on a date, or meet their friends at a movie. Live stage theatre, concerts, and opera performances all are comparatively expensive to produce. In many instances, the organizations that produce them face difficult challenges economically. Still opera survives, concerts sell out, and hopeful theatregoers wait for months for tickets to some Broadway plays. A governmental policy that may provide a subsidy to someone going to a performance at the Metropolitan Opera, but not to a person at home listening to a CD, is capricious. Government has absolutely no interest in what citizens watch or listen to, or through what communications media or performance venues they find aesthetic pleasure.

I can listen to a recorded string quartet in Gallatin Gateway, Montana, which is what I am doing as I write this sentence. I can also listen to that quartet at three in the morning if I wish. All recording technology liberates, while, at the same time, that liberation may challenge specific artists and certain arts. Many people argue that the fine arts inevitably are endangered by the popular ones. Cultural forms, however, continue to flourish so long as individuals support them. I cannot count the number of times that I have phoned for tickets to a major performance immediately after those tickets have gone on sale only to find out that the event is already sold out. Television enjoys great popularity, but people still read. In the United States alone more than 10,000 periodicals are published annually, in addition to more than 40,000 new book titles. During the 1980s the number of bookstores in the United States doubled and the number of books sold in them increased by thirty percent.[8] Some arts presenters find it difficult to survive; others thrive.

All this is part of the abundance provided by that salutary combination of affluence, technology, and liberty. Culture in a democratic society is organic–its forms develop and its directions grow in response to demographic shifts, technological innovations, and evolving taste. It is a nasty conceit of modern democracy that perceptions of taste, at heart, really have so much to do with judgments about propriety, behavior, and human worth. The smug proponents of public spending on the arts gingerly position themselves to overlook entirely just how much of this spending amounts to an upper-middle-class taste subsidy with accompanying bureaucratic costs. Justifying the taking of tax dollars from African American women in Houston who like gospel music, or from ranchers in Montana who like country music, to subsidize the affluent audience at the Metropolitan Opera in New York boggles the mind. And what is even more perplexing is the question of whether anyone defending the spending of public monies on the arts really believes that what art and culture looks like thirty years from now will thus be changed. Artistically and culturally people are voting constantly, with their wallets, their feet, and their remote controls.

Art in the twentieth century has been framed by two separate events, each of which occurred in Paris. In 1895, the first motion pictures were projected for a public audience. The movies were an art form in which production was collaborative and reproduction of the work was mechanical. Their arrival hearkened an undermining of the aesthetic of virtuosity while simultaneously providing cheap and easy access to drama, comedy, and documentary for everyone. Twenty-two years later in 1917, not far from where the first motion pictures had been presented, the painter Marcel Duchamp placed a stained urinal in an art exhibition as a piece of sculpture. This act assaulted the idea that a work of art was something unique and transcendent as our western aesthetic of virtuosity had so long maintained.

Between the advent of the movies and the death of art as Western civilization had known it lay fertile ground for a transformed understanding of all those phenomena that we label art. As it turns out, however, both learned and popular thinking has ignored such an understanding. Instead, aesthetic education and learned talk about culture creates false claims about the nature of art, nonsensical attempts to discriminate between high and popular culture, and widespread myths about how motion pictures and television actually function. By misunderstanding the media arts, society has opened itself further to fanciful theories about their effects.

Life does not imitate art in some strange and destructive fashion as the critics of television maintain. The notion that fiction drives how reality is perceived and lived is empty. To paraphrase one of today's leading theorists of performance, Richard Schechner, to think of a dramatic role as a person is like trying to have a picnic on a landscape painting.[9]

Television's form is its patterning and its repetition. The fact that television is used in a habitual manner means that the attitude with which we watched it is casual, even careless. There is no evidence that television has increased the social significance of the fictional. In a world of continuous transmission of TV programming, on multiple channels, twenty-four hours a day, there is no reason for us to conjure up a fear of its images competing for the allegiance of our souls. The TV picture is not akin to the pictographs that humans stenciled upon the walls of their caves in the hope of bountiful hunting. By becoming commonplace, the pictures, images, and sounds of the media arts have surrendered most of their power to the reasoning and critical sensitivity of any person into whose midst they come.

Virtuosity is based upon uniqueness. Repetition is based upon abundance. A copy of a Picasso painting that is well executed may provide a viewer just as much pleasure as the original. The original, however, is the work that has value in keeping with the aesthetic of virtuosity. The aesthetic of repetition shifts attention to what an audience member receives, and, hence, away from the uniqueness of the talent that created the work. During the 1960s, as he produced works based upon the repetition of well-known pictorial images such as Campbell's soup cans or Marilyn Monroe's face, the artist Andy Warhol coined a clever phrase that expressed what this changing reality would mean for culture and society. The notion that in the future everyone would be famous for fifteen minutes accords with the triumph of an aesthetic of repetition and with the democratization of culture.

Democracy is easily susceptible to corruption, the bickering of special interests, and the banality of elected officials who follow the latest polls. Democracies are inefficient. Leadership in them frequently provides scant commitment to deeper ideas, and often results in tawdry characters abusing high office. To paraphrase Winston Churchill, democracy is the worst form of government that one can imagine, except for all the others!

The same may be said of capitalism as an economic system. The forces of the market are unpredictable and irrational. Differences between the wealthy and the poor become exaggerated. The passions fueling competition become inflamed. The shoddiest goods, the poorest services, and the most exploitative business practices are likely to prevail because they are the most profitable. To which one answers, in lockstep with Churchill, that, indeed, capitalism is the worst economic system one can imagine, except for all the others!

In the marketplace, artistic abundance has thrived. At the dawn of the twenty-first century, practically no one must go to sleep starved for drama, comedy, fantasy or music. The argument that government still has some special calling to provide for our artistic diversions in such a world reflects a desperate confusion, both about the proper role and purpose of the state and about the evolving nature of art and individual aesthetic experience.

For over a decade, I have been a producer/director for a PBS affiliate. Through those years, I have also served periodically as a pitchman for the station during its pledge drives. On such occasions I am scripted to say that fewer than one out of every ten viewers of public television contributes to the station's support. I can only conclude that the other nine viewers of public television are quite content to leave it to their fellow taxpayers to subsidize their viewing of *Masterpiece Theater*, *The Boston Pops*, and *Lawrence Welk*.

As Laurence Jarvik points out in his analysis of public television entitled *PBS: Behind the Screen* (1997), public broadcasting has become a prisoner of its own cultural pretensions. It cuts deals with media giants like *Reader's Digest* and Turner Entertainment, courts corporate underwriters who suspiciously resemble advertisers, and does what all successful media businesses do by defining and developing a viewer culture that is uniquely its own. Public television in the United States for decades has been working at identifying and serving a niche audience.[10] Privately owned channels such as Discovery, A&E, The History Channel, and The Learning Channel have emerged and are proving to be successful by targeting specific segments of the market that PBS has identified for them. Even that veteran of public broadcasting, Garrison Keillor, admits: "I don't think there's any reason for public television to exist anymore . . . There isn't anything that they do that can't be done and done better by any one of a dozen cable channels. What C-Span is now is what public television should have been and never had the wit to do."[11]

Over the centuries, political regimes have demonstrated interest in supporting art for two reasons: self-aggrandizement for officialdom and propaganda. The measure of art in a democracy must be human pleasure. The great art forms in the United States—film, television, and popular music—have thrived in a competitive market system. Only a competitive market system that is as free as possible from both government subsidy and regulation can provide for individual tastes to be satisfied most equitably. The market system also provides the best means for encouraging and stimulating creativity. Art and culture are varied, prolific, abundant, and widespread. Nowhere and at no time in history have men and women of artistic talent been so well recognized and rewarded as they are in the film, television, and music industries of the United States.

NOTES

1. Herbert Gans, *Popular Culture and High Culture: An Analysis and Evaluation of Taste*, (New York: Basic Books, 1974), is a rare attempt to write seriously about taste, although it is now dated.

2. Jeremy Bentham's laissez-faire attitudes and views on the pursuit of the greatest good for the greatest number provide extraordinary insight into society and self-interest. See, *The Works of Jeremy Bentham* (New York: Russel & Russel, 1962).

3. Nick Gillespie, "Artistic Licenses," *Reason*, April, 1995, pp. 6, 7.

4. Sheldon Hackney, "NEH: What We Really Do," *The Washington Post National Weekly Edition*, September 25 - October 1, 1995, p. 29.

5. Quoted in *Transitions*, a video production of Channel Four (Great Britain) and WDR (Germany), 1986.

6. See the review of Rosentraub's book by Rick Henderson, *Reason*, August/September, 1997.

7. Reported on *Nightline*, ABC Television, July 4, 1995.

8. W. Russell Neuman, *The Future of the Mass Audience* (Cambridge: Cambridge University Press, 1991), p. 37.

9. Richard Schechner, *Performance Theory* (New York: Routledge, 1988), p. 165.

10. Charles Paul Freund, "The Prisoner," *Reason*, June, 1997.

11. Garrison Keillor, quoted in *The Nation*, January 5, 1998.

10

What Everyone Must Know About Television

With TV, you have let neither a demon nor a savior into your home. The set itself is only an appliance. On it you receive picture and sound that exploits intimacy to some degree. Watching regularly, you may develop a sense of connection with someone on the little screen. The virtuosity of the artists and technicians who produce TV programs, however, is concealed in the production process. As an art form television is lacking in power, except for the fact that it transcends time and space. Nowadays this is so taken for granted that no one pays much attention to it. TV is easy to access and is continuous in nature. For the user, after the initial investment of buying a set, TV is very inexpensive to watch.

Since the 1960s, theorists of the media and the arts increasingly have attributed the changes occurring in society and culture to what I call the forces of "technological determinism." This line of thinking has been underscored by attempts to analyze TV that have promoted misconceptions about the medium. Such thinking sees in television a mechanism that overwhelms human thought, sensibility, and will. W. Russell Neuman of the Annenberg School of Communication at the University of Pennsylvania points out that during the second half of the twentieth century both media and arts criticism have been dominated by Marxists. Trying to explain what they consider to be "the false consciousness of public enthusiasm for capitalist democracies," such critics "have attributed spectacular powers of persuasion to the mass media."[1]

Such thinking, moreover, long ago seeped outside the halls of our universities and now informs popular opinion extensively. In addition, as Marxism proper has waned, the notion of technological determinism has gradually replaced the classic Marxist idea that history was determined by the clash of antagonistic social classes. As a result, the term exploitation has been broadened from describing the relationship between the wealthy owners of the means of production and their hapless workers to a theory accounting for the psychological and cultural undermining of the masses. In this process, television has become a leading scapegoat to which to attribute social and cultural ills.

Interestingly, this sort of thinking has not been limited to researchers, thinkers, and critics identified solely with the Left. Much the same argument is taken up, for example, by a conservative critic of popular culture like Michael Medved. In his popular 1992 book, *Hollywood vs. America*, although he avoids faulting specific movies, TV programs, or popular songs for particular incidents or crimes, Medved generally attributes to American popular culture the undermining of society.[2] Among politicians, Patrick Buchanan talks about popular culture in America as "poisoning the well," hence conjuring up the image of a medieval village where everyone congregates at the same communal drinking source.

The classic complaint against television was that its message was monolithic and driving people toward becoming tribal. Although critics did not always say so, the threat of the medium was, in essence, fascistic. In the 1990s, however, much criticism of television has shifted away from this past wisdom. Consider, for example, the assertion by political communications theorist Roderick Hart that TV is undermining popular support for centralized power and politicians because "politics is now overexposed" and "television does not know how to reverence authority."[3] From this perspective, television is being faulted for offering its viewers too much. Television is bewildering the populace with abundance and choice. This criticism turns away from the fear of fascism toward the claim that television's impact is nothing short of anarchistic. Longtime television news commentator Daniel L. Schorr, who has moved to National Public Radio, argues: "The premise of my work has been that better communications would lead to better understanding, but it hasn't worked out that way. The communications revolution has provided faster and better means to spread confusion, misunderstanding, and, often, incitement."[4]

Television appeared at a crucial point in an ongoing transformation that has uprooted the notion of what we have held art to be for the past five centuries. It has also spread worldwide at the same time that a global transformation of economic and political life has occurred. The world's economy has become truly global since the 1970s and the quest for popular sovereignty is on the rise everywhere. Our ways of explaining social and political change, moreover, increasingly have come under serious challenge. Toward the end of the 1980s who would have predicted the collapse of communism in Eastern Europe leading to the break up of the Soviet Union itself? At the beginning of the 1990s who would have predicted the peaceful agreement by the minority white government in South Africa to constitutional reforms resulting in elections that swept the country's best known Black political prisoner into its presidency? In December 1989, a month after the Berlin Wall fell, I participated in a conference held at Rauisholzhausen, Germany. Every one of the forty prominent scholars, communications experts, sociologists, political scientists, and historians in attendance, was certain that Germany would not be reunited in our lifetime. Ten months later that unification was complete.

From a perspective that shifts to fit the circumstances, television is widely held culpable for nearly everything that is undesirable. If society is perceived to be marching in mindless lockstep, TV is the reason. If citizens are perceived to have become unduly critical of politicians and public institutions, TV is the reason. Crime on the rise–blame TV. The standardized test scores of high school seniors falling–it's TV's fault.

Occasionally, a contrary voice comes along. New York University's Henry J. Perkinson, the author of *Getting Better: Television and Moral Progress* (1991), presents himself as "rejecting the determinism inherent in most studies of the effects of television." Nonetheless, he winds up arguing that "television did facilitate changes we have made in our culture over the last thirty years."[5] Although much is promising about Perkinson's approach, while maintaining that he will not indulge in technological determinism, he does so in spite of himself. He uses the word "facilitate" instead of "cause." He gives TV viewers a lot more credit for discernment and judgment than most others do, but, finally, Perkinson winds up with these conclusions: Civil rights and improved race relations–thank TV; feminism and gender equity–thank TV; healthy skepticism toward the authority of science–TV is it; the U.S. military withdrawing from Viet Nam–thank TV; exposing Watergate–TV again!

Perkinson lines up everything he likes and gives TV credit for it, which mirrors in reverse how the far more numerous critics of television draw a bead on everything they find disturbing and blame television for it. But television is full of ambiguity. It is always a vessel to be filled with each individual's imagination, intent, understanding, purpose, and will. Even the comparatively straightforward news and informational programs on TV provide us no clear answers as to what watching them will necessarily "cause" or "facilitate."

Nowhere does TV have given effects on any viewer that can be established in advance. Even with regard to what we take to be the most susceptible of audiences for TV, namely children, this is not the case. Researchers George Comstock and Haejung Park begin their exhaustive summary of research on TV and children: "The stereotype of the child fixated by the continuous imagery is *false* (my italics) . . . *viewing* (their italics) in fact deconstructs into . . . content differences, program preferences, involvement, monitoring, and cognitive activity, social circumstances, and indiscriminate viewing."[6]

Still, other notions prevail. Numerous educators and parents recite the mantra that television causes children to be unimaginative. Television takes away, they maintain, the ability to conjure up images from deep inside oneself. Many critics are convinced that people who have grown up in the past several decades suffer from diminished capacities for creative thinking and imagination. This sounds very ominous, but it also sounds very familiar. This contemporary argument about TV echoes the words of the German Marxist, Walter Benjamin, reacting in the late 1930s to what he believed to be the similar destructiveness of the film age. "Our thoughts," Benjamin maintained, "have been replaced by images."[7]

Over the years, of course, numerous researchers have not passed up the opportunity to generate data in the hope of providing support to claims such as these. Even though imagination and creativity are especially slippery notions that are difficult to measure and assess, serious-minded research has been based on them. What such studies have to tell us, however, is sorely limited. A child watches a TV program and then is given a test or a task that the experimenter believes requires unusually imaginative or creative processes to perform. Yet, even the most dedicated researchers in this field admit to finding their results from such studies to be inconclusive.[8]

Nonetheless, this kind of research has unearthed some important bits of information. Children, for example, are observed not to really *watch* a television program like *Mr. Roger's Neighborhood* even though they comprehend and remember its contents quite well. Their attention to what is on the screen actually is haphazard and fleeting, although they evidently still are listening carefully.[9] During the 1980s, one set of observational studies measuring the differences between watching television, reading a book, and listening to radio, concluded that the purely auditory radio experience best stimulated children's imagination and retention of information. That study concluded that book reading came in a distant third![10]

Speculation that attributes educational decline in the United States to television is rampant. There is, of course, evidence that America's public education has deteriorated at a startling rate. Not the least of these indicators are the declining SAT (Scholastic Aptitude Test) scores achieved by high school seniors. Aggregate verbal and quantitative scores on them have gone down nearly eighty points since the end of the 1960s.[11] Television, however, was widely used in the United States *before* the SAT scores started to go down. At the beginning of the 1960s Americans on average already were watching television for more than five hours a day. Even in the 1990s teenagers on average watch TV no more than three hours a day.[12] The amount of television watched by teenagers in the United States has changed very little over nearly four decades. Teen viewing of TV is steadily measured at around half the average for the population as a whole, and teenage girls are the demographic group in the entire population that watches TV the least. For them, why not argue that shopping at the mall or talking on the telephone causes a decline in test scores?

What I find singularly lacking in speculation on the relationship of TV to learning, let alone to such slippery classifications as creativity or imagination, is a comparative perspective. Television is global and the programming available on it everywhere is similar. Habits of watching television among school age populations around the globe are similar, but the precipitous decline in educational performance is not. In fact, we really know that American education is in so much trouble when we see comparisons to pupils and schools in other countries. Teenagers in Japan and Italy actually watch slightly more TV on average than do their American counterparts, but that does not mean that academic performance in those countries has declined as it has in the United States. As a 1995 report by the independent Paris-based International Organization for Economic Cooperation concluded: "Viewed in an international perspective, the average achievement scores of American children range from mediocre to poor, depending on the subject matter. . . . While it is true that American schools do a particularly poor job of educating Blacks and Hispanics, one should not conclude that students in middle-class suburbs are uniformly well-served. In mathematics and science . . . the nation's top students rank far behind less elite samples of students from other countries."[13]

In spite of the global spread of television, academic standards for adolescents are being upheld elsewhere. Academic performance still is valued at the high school level throughout most of the world. In the United States, high school is the weakest link in a deteriorating system of public education. Insofar as academic learning, intellectual challenge, and the mastery of basic information is concerned, high school in the United States has become a *missing link*.

Nearly anyone acquainted with the public high schools in America can embark upon enumerating their failings. One fundamental fault with them, however, resides in the deeply ingrained attitude spreading broadly across American culture that adolescence is a time for fun and not for demanding scholastic work. Personal development, according to this widely accepted view, is held to be not only distinct from intellectual development but also to be at odds with it. This attitude arose in the late 1950s and became widespread and dominant by the late 1960s.[14] Anyone wishing to account for the perilous decline of high school education in the United States, must come back to the question: "Just what does our society want from this institution?" My answer is that it wants to provide conditions that are assumed to maximize pleasant adolescent peer experiences unblemished by the intrusion of academic demands.

American high school pupils are meant to feel good about themselves. Standards of academic performance create unhealthy forms of competition for them. Hard and serious work for the mind interferes with the fun of growing up. Being told that you should feel good about yourself has supplanted the truth that a person feels good about achievements that are real. For children who attend our better and safer high schools, and who come from reasonably stable and caring homes, the result is a "dumbing down."[15] More often than not that eventually will be compensated for by the experience of higher education. For others from less promising backgrounds who are flushed through one of America's typical high schools, the results are devastating.

During the recent past, much of the educational damage done by high schools in the United States has been compensated for by a college or university education for many students. But the superiority of American higher education is also starting to erode. Attitudes toward learning that dominate our high schools are spreading to the nation's campuses. Moreover, young people in the population who are most at risk, and the most in need of a solid educational basis from high school to carry them through life, are the least likely to ever see the halls of higher education.

Nonetheless, in the United States we have made it seem as if everyone must go to college. In 1995, for the first time in the nation's history the number of students attending colleges and universities actually exceeded the number of pupils attending high schools.[16] A high school diploma has become meaningless in the United States, even though this is not the world's view. In the United States we squander the social and cultural potential of adolescence by having a public high school system that is bankrupt. And while American higher education is vast and many institutions within it are committed to some form of excellence, the quality of education at many colleges and universities is eroding under the pressure of burgeoning numbers of ill-prepared students. As the cost of higher education escalates and the federal government offers more financial inducements for more students to attend college, the problems only increase. The nation's colleges have begun graduating thousands of individuals who face staggering amounts of debt accumulated as undergraduates. These graduates, moreover, often are poorly educated in the basics of knowledge, as well as having a poor or non-existent preparation for any specific career field.

There is not a scintilla of evidence that television has caused the steady decline in American education. The real causes are the failed educational and government policies that create or contribute to the bloat and waste found in the administration of schools, colleges, and universities, warped and misplaced priorities that erode learning, the tyranny of worthless courses required for certification to teach in the public schools, and the proliferation of empty educational dogma. Social promotion and the indulgence of trendy social fads have entirely undermined standards of merit and performance in the high schools. Open admissions and grade inflation undermine higher education. The decline of public education in the United States comes neither from prime-time TV nor from the Saturday morning 'toons, but rather from the failures of the policy makers and the educators to whom society has entrusted it.

Public education in the United States is not only ineffective and in disarray, it is also costly. Per student expenditures in both primary and secondary schools in the United States exceed those in nations such as Germany, Japan, Great Britain, France, and Italy. Expenditures escalate, teacher salaries rise, teacher-to-pupil ratios are lowered, and high school dropout rates decline.[17] The product, nonetheless, keeps getting worse. Many of America's high school graduates cannot find Massachusetts or Missouri on a map. Their basic use of English is mangled in inarticulate speech and tortured writing. Numbers of high school graduates cannot read well enough to fill out a job application. The day may not be that far off when much the same will be said of plenty of individuals holding baccalaureate degrees.

People, by and large, do what society expects of them. So long as we have a consensus in our culture that sets no real academic standards in high schools, that inflates grades, and that promotes children and adolescents from one grade to the next on grounds having nothing to do with the levels of learning that they have achieved, then we will continue to have miserable schools.

Societies reap what they sow. Set standards low, reward children, adolescents, and young adults simply to make them feel good about themselves, and the result will be the mess that we have in American education today. Then further fuel this problem with political rhetoric that calls for assuring every American a chance to attend college and a similar decline of standards in higher education assuredly will follow.

Educational reform can come only from redirecting the philosophies and policies of schools. The encouragement of competition among schools can be increased by making tuition vouchers and tax credits available to lower income parents and students to use at any schools or colleges that they wish to attend. In itself, such a scheme will not solve all of the problems, but a healthy dose of competition for the worst of our public schools is long overdue. Education in America may be too vast to be entirely privatized, but it also too important to be left entirely in the hands of the educationists whose warped theories of learning and society have undermined it. Breaking the tyranny of grade inflation and social promotion likely will prove difficult, for the lassitude and misguided generosity on which they are based comes from deep ideological sources. Public education requires radical reform.

But wait, some readers must be saying, the problems with American youth begin far earlier than adolescence and young adulthood, and is not television the culprit? What about young children being abandoned in front of a television set nearly every day? Anyone can conjure up just this picture in the mind's eye. The operable word here, however, is "abandonment" as it is used in a psychological sense. A child would do no better to be abandoned in the stacks of the Library of Congress or in one of the rooms of the Metropolitan Museum of Art. It is not the medium that matters; instead, it is the primary behavior through which the medium is given its context. Emotional neglect is the problem, not where you happen to be placed when that neglect occurs. If you are a child with an irresponsible crackhead for a mother, you surely are better off spending the evening with *Roseanne* or *Murphy Brown* than with mom.

The people we are around and what those people say and do are our primary world. You do not become a runner for a drug dealer and wind up murdering a rival because you saw someone commit this act on TV. You become a criminal not only because you are in an environment in which crime is prevalent, but also because the people around you–whom you know and whom you trust–rationalize and justify crime. The root of human tragedy is intellectual error.

The erosion of primary relationships in the lives of many young people, and not the effects of the secondary ones that TV viewers supposedly have to fictional characters, is the root of social pathologies. Television does not cause illegitimacy. As one twenty-year-old, unmarried with two children born out-of-wedlock, testified before Congress: "It's not a big deal to get pregnant. I believe teenagers have babies for a variety of reasons, such as needing love, rebelling against authority and to feel grown up. . . . However, I feel that the overlying reason is because it is accepted by society. Our mothers, fathers, teachers, even our ministers, and especially our peers . . . accept the situation."[18] People are influenced by what the people around them think and believe. Specific government programs have provided additional fuel to the fires of illegitimacy: "What the welfare system does is enable a young woman to legitimately say to herself, 'If I have this baby I can support it without a husband.'"[19] Social misery may be attributed to family dysfunction, character disorder, self-destructive behavior, racism, eroded job opportunities in certain areas resulting from changes in the global economy, inferior schools, or failed government programs. Where the emphasis is placed and how the causal argument is pursued is a matter of political ideology. What is on television, however, does not cause social misery, nor does what is on television cause crime.

Crime has increased in most democracies worldwide toward the close of the twentieth century. There are many variables that relate to crime, but in the United States crime rates predictably rise and fall everywhere in direct proportion to the percentage of young adult males in the population. Remarkably, however, if drug and drug-related crimes in the United States were factored out, the crime picture would be transformed entirely. Half of the murders committed in this country are drug related. As many as three-quarters of the convicts in America's jails and prisons at any time are incarcerated for drug or drug-related crimes.[20]

Public policy and the enforcement of drug laws have become grossly warped and unproductive. For all the ferocity and expense that the United States has put into the war on drugs, it remains a bizarre and uneven undertaking. Sometimes letting people sell and use drugs in public. Sometimes seeing the police break down the doors of terrified citizens who know nothing about drugs. Sometimes automobiles, boats, airplanes, and other property being seized from people engaged in narcotics selling or money laundering. Sometimes cops take the drugs they have confiscated in a raid and sell them or consume them themselves. One state even concluded that in some jurisdictions, and for certain drugs, the Federal Drug Enforcement Agency had become the single biggest supplier of the drugs available on the street because of the agency's sting operations.

George Washington University law professor Paul Butler points out that arrests of African Americans for drug possession are vastly disproportionate to the estimates of drug use in that demographic group.[21] The enforcement of drug laws appears to be grossly inequitable and capricious, and even the legislation itself is often warped. There are vastly different penalties for the possession of crack cocaine, for example, as opposed to powdered cocaine, even though there is no pharmaceutical evidence of any real difference between the effects of these substances.[22] Drug policy and enforcement is completely out of control in the United States. Drug laws are trampling upon basic civil liberties and due process, while filling the jails and prisons with an array of "criminals." And still the sale and use of drugs goes on.

In his 1994 book *The Index of Leading Cultural Indicators* the former U.S. drug czar, William J. Bennett, cited a portion of a Congressional speech by United States Senator Daniel P. Moynihan of New York:

"In 1929 in Chicago during Prohibition, four gangsters killed seven gangsters on February 14. The nation was shocked. The event became legend. It merits not one but two entries in the *World Book Encyclopedia*. I leave it to others to judge, but it would appear that the society in the 1920s was simply not willing to put up with this degree of deviancy. In the end, the Constitution was amended, and Prohibition, which lay behind so much gangster violence, ended."[23] Bennett, however, cites Moynihan only to point out that the community was outraged. He ignores the precise and telling consequence of that outrage: the demise of the ill-conceived law that prohibited the production, sale, and serving of alcoholic beverages in the United States.

Opponents of decriminalizing narcotics in the United States refuse to recognize that the war on drugs is a repeat performance of Prohibition, and the broad social consequences of it have been similar. The United States has ended up with warring criminal bands battling for control over turf and drug markets. Of course, one thing is different; even if they consumed it illegally at a speakeasy, drinkers during Prohibition still were not forced to steal to buy their next beer! Illegal drugs today are so expensive, however, primarily because the trade in them is criminal.

The best argument against decriminalizing drugs is the numbers of new addicts that might be created were drugs available easily and cheaply. It is argued that this would be especially true for those in society most at risk: persons with the lowest self-esteem, the least hope, or the ones who simply are the most bored. But drugs are widely available now; they just cost a lot and the desire to purchase them brings people necessarily into criminal activity. Were drugs decriminalized and their sale regulated in a fashion similar to alcohol, crime in the United States would be substantially diminished.

To attribute the failure of our educational system, illegitimacy, or crime to television is nonsense. The reform of American society is vital, but such reform is only undermined by incorrectly placing the blame for social problems on TV. In part, this is an issue of misunderstanding the medium of TV, the nature of art, and the relationship of art to society and culture. In part, it is wishful thinking that if only the most pervasive communication medium were altered, then many of society's ills would magically be cured.

For many educators, politicians, and opinion makers, the continued promotion of the received ideas that have accumulated in public discourse is self-serving. Their perpetuation of inaccuracies about human nature and the realities of society provides payoffs. Some of these rewards are material; a lot of people have secured comfortable lives for themselves as employees and administrators in the failed institutions of American public life. Much of the payoff, however, is psychological and ideological. In the battle of ideas, we must come to terms with the widespread notion that life is an endless parade of victims. The most injurious consequence of this mind-set is the inevitable damage it does to human pride and self-assertiveness.

The repetition in television constitutes its art and its form. By contrast, the repetition of mistaken social and cultural tenets constitutes an assault upon the human spirit and its deepest longings for liberty, choice, and a genuine sense of self-worth. Two central issues confront society: (1) What is the proper role of the state? and (2) How can individual initiative, freedom, and choice be maximized? Only to the extent that public policy is pushed toward risk-taking that results in wide ranging educational reform and changes in American law to decriminalize activities that are not directly injurious to others can society be effectively redirected. To the extent that change is needed and reform is long overdue, it is because our educational system is poor and our laws are flawed. What's on television has nothing to do with it.

NOTES

1. W. Russell Neuman, *The Future of the Mass Audience* (Cambridge: Cambridge University Press, 1991), p. 28.

2. Michael Medved, *Hollywood vs. America* (New York: Harper Perennial, 1992), see especially the introductory chapter.

3. Roderick Hart, *Seducing America: How Television Charms the Modern Voter* (Oxford/New York: Oxford University Press, 1994), p. 75.

4. *Brandeis Review*, Summer, 1995, p. 18, reporting on Schorr's comments at the commencement exercises upon his receiving an Honorary Doctorate from Brandeis University, Waltham, Massachusetts. [My italics.]

5. Henry J. Perkinson, *Getting Better: Television and Moral Progress* (New Brunswick/London: Transaction Publishing, 1991), from the book jacket.

6. George Comstock and Haejung Park, *Television and the American Child* (New York/London/Sydney: Academic Press, 1991), p. 1.

7. Hart, *Seducing*, p. 85.

8. Dorothy G. Singer, "Creativity of Children in a Television World," in Gordon L. Berry and Joy Keiko Asamen, eds., *Children & Television* (Newbury Park, CA: Sage Publications, 1993), p. 85.

9. ibid., p. 81.

10. ibid., p. 81.

11. William J. Bennett, *The Index of Leading Cultural Indicators* (New York: Simon & Schuster, 1994), p. 82.

12. ibid., p. 103.

13. *National Review*, September 25, 1995, p. 14.

14. Landon Y. Jones, *Great Expectations* (New York: Ballantine Books, 1980) presents an excellent analysis of the demographic and economic basis for cultural change in the U.S. during the 1960s. The rise of teenage culture and new attitudes toward adolescence commands his special attention.

15. See Charles J. Sykes, *Dumbing Down Our Kids* (New York: St. Martin's Griffin, 1996).

16. Walter Williams, "More Money for What?" *The Washington Times*, February 22, 1997.

17. Bennett, *Index*, pp. 87-91.

18. Associated Press Release, "Congress Debates Welfare, Illegitimacy," March 2, 1995.

19. ibid.

20. Richard Clutterbuck, *Drugs, Crime and Corruption: Thinking the Unthinkable* (New York: New York University Press, 1995), p. 130.

21. Paul Butler on *Rivera Live*, June 14, 1997.

22. *Cochran and Company*, Court-TV, June 3, 1997.

23. Bennett, *Index*, p. 27.

Afterword

What is TV's place in history? What changes has TV wrought in the way humans live and in what they value and believe? Where do ideas come from and how do they spread? What are the driving forces in human behavior? Television provides touchstones that set us off upon the highways and byways of exploring any and all such questions. But television provides answers to none of them.

One phrase sticks in my mind that comes from a book by W. Russell Neuman, who writes: "There is no prospect of resurrecting the technologies, life-styles, and values of small town and rural society . . . *time's arrow does not suddenly reverse course.*"[1]   This challenges us to understand that we cannot repeat the past. On both the Left and the Right there are serious errors in believing that specific institutions and practices of the past can be preserved or resurrected whole. Flaws in these contemporary romanticisms, however, must not shroud the truth that core values still need to be clarified, articulated, cherished, and lived by.

The course of history is toward human liberty and self-actualization. And this course is not in conflict with civility, decency, and constructive social behavior. The key to social and cultural wisdom is in understanding what must change and what must stay the same. To the extent that the term the "age of television" may have been useful to us in the recent past, we must recognize that its value is exhausted. At base, the term was never accurate insofar as it implied that TV was a force that was determining the development of society and culture.

The purpose and goal of human development is to liberate the human mind and spirit, and to permit men and women to realize the fullness of their potential and their desires so long as doing so does not directly inflict harm upon others. Still, many people resist this fundamental truth. Some are those ideologues clinging to the idea that government is an end in its own right, and that the state, in one form or another, is the primary apparatus through which human happiness will be achieved. Some are the educators spouting received ideas devoid of any vision of challenge and excellence. For them, the concept of opportunity simply is incompatible with any form of meritocracy. Some are the parents and social theorists who avoid making tough-minded choices that guide young people toward a genuine sense of self-worth based upon hard work and accomplishment. Some are the narrow-minded in all walks of life who resist new technologies. Some are the citizens who demand cultural, social, and economic planning on the part of the state in attempts to preserve what is destined for the ash heap of history. Some are those who see democracy only as a mechanism to exert social control through repression by recourse to majority rule that violates fundamental human rights and liberties. Some are those who can conceive of government only as an apparatus for assuaging their own special interests, and who therefore abandon all principle for short-term benefits. Some are those who demonize television by misrepresenting its true nature and its use.

As in every era, transitions are difficult. Because today we are at the end of one long phase of history, the stakes look especially high. And because today's technologies of communication are global, new voices are being heard. It is the function of human reason to provide the on going basis for a society and a culture to thrive in liberty. Beyond all the deceptions that are perpetuated about television, our commitment must be to analyze and to accept this medium in accordance with the basic principles of rationality and freedom.

NOTE

1. W. Russell Neuman, *The Future of the Mass Audience* (Cambridge: Cambridge University Press, 1991), p. 9.

Bibliography

BOOKS CITED OR CONSULTED

Andrew, J. Dudley. *The Major Film Theories: An Introduction.* Oxford/New York: Oxford University Press, 1976.

Armstrong, Robert Plant. *The Affecting Presence: An Essay in Humanistic Anthropology.* Urbana/Chicago/London: University of Illinois Press, 1971.

——. *The Powers of Presence: Consciousness, Myth, and Affecting Presence.* Philadelphia: University of Pennsylvania Press, 1981.

——. *Wellspring: On the Myth and Source of Culture.* Berkeley: University of California Press, 1975.

Aronowitz, Stanley. *Dead Artists, Live Theories, and Other Cultural Problems.* New York: Routledge, 1994.

Bandura, Albert. *Social Learning.* Englewood Cliffs, NJ: Prentice Hall, 1968.

——. *Aggressions: A Social Learning Analysis.* Englewood Cliffs, NJ: Prentice Hall, 1973.

Bandura, Albert, and Richard H. Walters. *Social Learning and Personality Development.* New York: Holt, Rinehart, and Winston, Inc., 1963.

Barker, Martin, and Julian Petley, eds. *Ill Effects: The Media/Violence Debate.* London: Routledge, 1997.

Bennett, William. *The Index of Leading Cultural Indicators.* New York: Simon & Schuster, 1994.

Bentham, Jeremy. *The Works of Jeremy Bentham.* New York: Russel and Russel, 1962.

Berger, Arthur Asa. *Popular Culture Genres: Theories and Texts.* Newbury Park, CA: Sage, 1992.

Bergland, David. *Libertarianism in One Lesson,* 6th ed. Costa Mesa, CA: Orpheus, 1993.

Berry, Gordon L., and Joy Keiko Asamen, eds. *Children and Television*. Newbury Park, CA: Sage, 1993.

Bistray, Georges. *Marxist Models of Literary Realism*. New York: Columbia University Press, 1978.

Bryant, Jennings, and Dolf Zillmann, eds. *Perspectives on Media Effects*. Hillsdale, NJ: Lawrence Erlbaum Associates, 1986.

——. *Media Effects: Advances in Theory and Research*. Hillsdale, NJ: Lawrence Erlbaum Associates, 1994.

Clutterbuck, Richard. *Drugs, Crime, and Corruption: Thnking the Unthinkable*. New York: New York University Press, 1995.

Comstock, George, and Haejung Park. *Television and the American Child*. New York: Academic Press, 1991.

Cook, Pam, and Philip Dodd, eds. *Women and Film: A 'Sight and Sound' Reader*. Philadelphia: Temple University Press, 1993.

Cooper-Chen, Anne. *Games in the Global Village: A 50-Nation Study of Entertainment Television*. Bowling Green, OH: Bowling Green University Press, 1994.

Donner, Stanley T., ed. *The Meaning of Commercial Television*. Austin: University of Texas Press, 1967.

Donnerstein, Edward, Daniel Lenz, and Steven Penrod, eds. *The Question of Pornography: Research Findings and Policy Implications*. New York: The Free Press, 1987.

Ellul, Jacques, translated by M. J. O'Connell. *The Betrayal of the West*. New York: Seabury, 1978.

Ellul, Jacques, translated by John Wilkinson. *The Technological Society*. New York: Alfred Knopf, 1964.

Enzensberger, Hans Magnus, translated by Michael Roloff. *The Consciousness Industry*. New York: Seabury, 1974.

Featherstone, Mike. *Consumer Culture and Post-Modernism*. Newbury Park, CA: Sage, 1990.

Feuer, Lewis. *Marx and the Intellectuals*. New York: Anchor Books, 1969.

Fukuyama, Francis. *The End of History and the Last Man*. New York: Avon Books, 1992.

Gabler, Neal. *An Empire of Their Own: How the Jews Invented Hollywood*. New York: Crown Publishers, 1988.

Gans, Herbert. *Deciding What's News*. New York: Random House, 1980.

——. *Popular Culture and High Culture: An Analysis and Evaluation of Taste*. New York: Basic Books, 1974.

Gardiner, Gerald. *The Censorship Papers: Movie Censorship Letters from the Hays Office, 1934-1968*. New York: Dodd, Mead, 1987.

Gerbner, George, and Marsha Seiffert. *World Communications: A Handbook*. New York: Longman, 1984.

Gerbner, George, Robert Heigh, and Richard Byrne, eds. *Communications in the 21st Century*. New York: Wiley, 1981.

Goodwin, Andrew. *Dancing in the Distraction Factory: Music, Television, and Popular Culture*. Minneapolis: University of Minnesota Press, 1992.

Greenfield, Patricia Marks. *Mind and Media: The Effects of Television, Video Games, and Computers*. Cambridge: Harvard University Press, 1984.

Grossberg, Lawrence, Cary Nelson, and Paula Treichler, eds. *Cultural Studies*. New York: Routledge, 1992.

Hart, Roderick. *Seducing America: How Television Charms the Modern Voter*. Oxford/New York: Oxford University Press, 1994.

Himmelstein, Hal. *On the Small Screen: New Approaches in Television and Video Criticism*. New York: Praeger, 1981.

Holub, Robert C. *Reception Theory: A Critical Introduction*. London: Methuen, 1984.

Jarvie, Ian C. *Movies as Social Criticism*. Metuchen, NJ: Scarecrow Publishers, 1978.

Jauss, Hans Robert, translated by Timothy Bahti. *Toward an Aesthetic of Reception*. Minneapolis: University of Minnesota Press, 1982.

Jones, Landon Y. *Great Expectations: America and the Baby Boom Generation*. New York: Ballantine, 1980.

Jowett, Garth, et al., eds. *Children and the Movies: Media Influence and the Payne Fund Controversy*. Cambridge: Cambridge University Press, 1996.

Jowett, Garth, and James M. Linton. *Movies as Mass Communication*. Beverly Hills: Sage, 1980.

Jowett, Garth, and Victoria O'Donnell. *Propaganda and Persuasion*, 2nd ed. Newbury Park, CA/London/New Delhi: Sage, 1992.

Kinder, Marsha. *Playing with Power in Movies, Television, and Video Games: From Muppet Babies to Teenage Mutant Ninja Turtles*. Berkeley/Los Angeles: University of California Press, 1991.

Lev, Peter. *The Euro-American Cinema*. Austin: The University of Texas Press, 1993.

Lewis, Lisa. *Gender Politics and MTV: Voicing the Difference*. Philadelphia: Temple University Press, 1990.

Liebes, Tamar, and Elihu Katz. *The Export of Meaning: Cross-Cultural Readings of 'Dallas'*. Oxford/New York: Oxford University Press, 1990.

Lull, James. *Media, Communication, Culture: A Global Approach*. New York: Columbia University Press, 1995.

Malamuth, Neil, and Edward Donnerstein, eds. *Pornography and Sexual Aggression*. New York: Academic Press, 1986.

McCabe, Colin, ed. *High Theory/Low Culture*. Manchester, U.K.: Manchester University Press, 1986.

McGuire, William J. "The Myth of Massive Media Impact: Savagings and

Salvagings." In George Comstock, ed., *Public Communication and Behavior*. Orlando: Academic Press, 1986, pp. 173-257.

McLuhan, Marshall. *Understanding Media: The Extensions of Man*. New York: Signet Books, 1964.

McLuhan, Marshall, and Bruce R. Powers, eds. *The Global Village: Transformations in World Life and Media in the 21st Century*. Oxford/New York: Oxford University Press, 1989.

Medved, Michael. *Hollywood vs. America*. New York: Harper Perennial, 1992.

Michel, Hevre, and Anne-Laure Angoulvent. *Les Télévisions en Europe*. Paris: Presses Universitaire de France, 1992.

Moley, Raymond. *The Hays Office*. New York: Bobbs-Merrill, 1945.

Monaco, Paul. *Cinema and Society: France and Germany During the 1920's*. New York/Amsterdam: Elsevier, 1976.

——. *Modern European Culture and Consciousness 1870-1980*. Albany, NY: State University of New York Press, 1983.

——. *Ribbons in Time: Movies and Society Since 1945*. Bloomington/Indianapolis: Indiana University Press, 1987.

Moores, Shaun. *Interpreting Audiences: The Ethnography of Media Consumption*. Newbuty Park, CA/London/New Delhi: Sage, 1993.

Murray, John P. *Television and Youth: Twenty-Five Years of Research and Controversy*. Stanford, CA: The Boys Town Center for The Study of Youth Development, 1980.

National Television Violence Study (Executive Summary), Vol. 1, March, 1996. Santa Barbara, CA: The Center for Communication and Social Policy.

National Television Violence Study (Executive Summary), Vol. 2, March, 1997. Santa Barbara, CA: The Center for Communication and Social Policy.

Neuman, W. Russell. *The Future of the Mass Audience*. Cambridge: Cambridge University Press, 1991.

Newcomb, Horace. *Television: The Critical View*. Oxford/New York: Oxford University Press, 1983.

Ong, Walter J. *Orality and Literacy: The Technologizing of the Word*. London: Methuen, 1982.

O'Sullivan, Tim, et al., ed. *Key Concepts in Communication and Cultural Studies*. New York: Routledge, 1994.

Penley, Constance, ed. *Feminism and Film Theory*. New York: Routledge, 1988.

Perkinson, Henry J. *Getting Better: Television and Moral Progress*. New Brunswick, NJ/London: Transaction Publishing, 1991.

Postman, Neil. *Amusing Ourselves to Death: Public Discourse in the Age of Show Business*. New York/London: Penguin USA, 1986.

——. *Technopoly: The Surrender of Culture to Technology*. New York: Alfred Knopf, 1992.

Real, Michael R. *Exploring Media Culture: A Guide*. Thousand Oaks/London/New Delhi: Sage, 1996.

Rowe, David. *Popular Cultures: Rock Music, Sport, and the Politics of Pleasure*. Thousand Oaks/London/New Delhi: Sage, 1995.

Rusher, William A. *The Coming Battle for the Media: Curbing the Power of the Media Elite*. New York: Morrow, 1988.

Schechner, Richard. *Performance Theory*. New York: Routledge, 1988.

Seligman, Martin E. P. *Helplessness: On Depression, Development, and Death*. San Francisco: W.H. Freeman Co., 1975.

——. *Learned Optimism: How to Change Your Mind and Your Life*. New York: Simon and Schuster Pocket Books, 1990.

Signorielli, Nancy. *Mass Media Images and Their Impact on Health*. Westport, CT: Greenwood, 1993.

Signorielli, Nancy, Elizabeth Miche, and Carol Katzman, eds. *Role Portrayal and Stereotyping on Television*. Westport, CT: Greenwood, 1985.

Sowell, Thomas. *Inside American Education: The Decline, The Deception, The Dogma*. New York/Oxford/Singapore/Sydney: The Free Press, 1993.

Strossen, Nadine. *Defending Pornography: Free Speech, Sex, and the Fight for Women's Rights*. New York: Charles Scribner & Sons, 1995.

Sykes, Charles J. *Dumbing Down Our Kids*. New York: St. Martin's Griffin, 1996.

Thompson, John B. *Ideology and Modern Culture: Critical Social Theory in the Era of Mass Communication*. Cambridge, U.K.: Polity Press, 1990.

Tyler, Parker. *Magic and Myth of the Movies*. New York: H. Holt & Co., 1947

Van Zoonen, Lisbet. *Feminist Media Studies*. Thousand Oaks/London/New Delhi: Sage, 1994.

Wartella, Ellen A. *The Carroll C. Arnold Distinguished Lecture: The Context of Television Violence*. Needham Heights, MA: Allyn and Bacon, 1997.

ARTICLES, PAPERS, AND PROGRAMS CITED

Andrews, Edward L. "Court Upholds Ban on Indecent Broadcasting Programming." *The New York Times*, July 1, 1995.

Associate Press Release. "Congress Debates Welfare, Illegitimacy." March 2, 1995.

Barnes, Fred. "Insurrection." *The New Republic*, June 22, 1992.

Bellafante, Ginia. "What's On in Tokyo?" *Time*, Feb. 16, 1996.

Blumenthal, Sidney. "Dan's Big Plans." *Vanity Fair*, September, 1992.

Bowman, James. "Too Much Mr. Nice Guy." *The National Review*, June 22, 1992.

Bozeman Daily Chronicle, The, July 15, 1994.

Brandeis Review, Summer, 1995.

Carter, Bill. "Stern Reportedly Rules Out Late-Night Talk Show." *The New York Times*, January 5, 1994.

Cochran and Company. Court-TV, June 3, 1997.

Corry, John. "Fairness Most Foul." *The American Spectator*, Nov., 1995.

Cronin, Michael W. "Oral Communication Across the Curriculum." Seminar, Montana State University, Bozeman, May 12, 1997.

The Economist, January 25, 1992.

Freund, Charles Paul. "The Prisoner." *Reason*, June, 1997.

Gabler, Neil. "Endangered Species." *George Magazine*, May, 1997.

Gartner, Michael. "O.J. Circus, Blame TV." *USA Today*, Oct. 3, 1995.

Garvey, John. "Commercials." *Commonweal*, February 10, 1995.

Gelernter, David. "The Real Story of Orenthal James." *The National Review*, October 9, 1995.

Gillespie, Nick. "Artistic Licenses." *Reason*, April, 1995.

———. "Chip Off the Block." *Reason*, November, 1995.

Gladwell, Malcolm. "Cheap Thrills: There's More to TV Than V. There's Also T." *The New Yorker*, April 19, 1997.

Guilleband, Jean-Claude. "A Mysterious Medium." *Unesco Courier*, October, 1992.

Hackney, Sheldon. "NEH: What We Really Do." *The Washington Post National Weekly Edition*, September 25 - October, 1, 1995.

Hanson, Christopher. "Media Bashing." *Columbia Journalism Review*, November/December, 1992.

Horn, Miriam. "Teaching Television Violence." *U.S. News and World Report*, December 27, 1993.

Howard, Gerald. "Divide and Deride: Prevalence of Stupidity in the Mass Media." *The Nation*, December 20, 1993.

Hynds, Patricia. "Balancing Bias in the News: Critical Questions Can Help Viewers." *Media and Values*, Fall, 1992.

Katz, Jon. "Beavis and Butt-head." *Rolling Stone*, March 24, 1995.

Lentini, Nina. "Stop Wasting Money Researcher Tells TV Advertisers." *Adweek*, April 17, 1989.

Lewis, Michael. "The Boy in the Bubble." *The New Republic*, October 19, 1992.

Logan, Michael. "Wheel of Fortune Sends in the Clones." *TV Guide*, October 26 - November 1, 1991.

Lowry, Brian. "Study Finds Improvement in Handling On-Air Violence." *Los Angeles Times*, January 14, 1998.

Meadows, Donella H. "We Are What We Watch." *The Baltimore Sun,* September 28, 1994.

McCombs, Maxwell E. and D. L. Shaw. "The Agenda-Setting Function of the Mass Media." *Public Opinion Quarterly*, 36, 1976.

McConnell, Frank. "Art Is Dangerous: Beavis and Butt-head, for Example."
     Commonweal, January 14, 1994.

The Nation, January 5, 1998.

The National Review, September 25, 1995.

The Newshour With Jim Lehrer. PBS, April 7, 1997.

The New York Times, November 11, 1993.

——. November 24, 1993.

Nightline. ABC-TV, July 4, 1995.

Rivera Live. CNBC, June 14, 1997.

Rogers, Everett M. "When the Media Have Strong Effects: Intermedia Pro-
     cesses." Paper, SCA National Conference, San Diego, November, 1996.

Rosenthal, Andrew. "Quayle's Moment." *The New York Times*, July 3, 1992.

Showbiz Story Page, March 26, 1997

Slansky, Paul and Steve Radlauer. "Airhead Apparent." *Esquire*, August, 1992.

Solomon, Jolie. "Mickey's Trip to Trouble." *Newsweek*, February 14, 1994.

Time Magazine, June 5, 1995.

Transitions. Channel Four (GB) and WDR (Germany), 1986.

U.S. News and World Report, November 1, 1993.

Valente, Judith. "Do You Believe What Newspeople Tell You?" *Parade
     Magazine*, March 2, 1997.

Variety, July 27, 1960.

——. December 13, 1961.

Volkoh, Alexander. "How Green Is Our Valley?" *Reason*, March, 1995.

Walker, Martin. "Disney's Saccharin Turns Sour." *World Press Review*, March,
     1994.

The Washington Post National Weekly Edition, January 26, 1998.

Williams, Walter. "More Money for What?" *The Washington Times*, February
     22, 1997.

Wilson, Samuel H. "Disney Dissonance." *Natural History*, December, 1994.

Zoglin, Richard. "If Not the Jetsons, What?" *Time*, March 22, 1993.

——. "Sitcom Politics." *Time*, September 21, 1992.

Index

About the Author

PAUL MONACO is the Department Head of Media & Theatre Arts and Professor of Cinema/Video at Montana State University, Bozeman. He is the author of several books on the cinematic arts and the history of culture, as well as a filmmaker and video producer. As a producer/director for Montana Public Television, he has been responsible for numerous productions that have shown on public television both regionally and nationally. Among these productions are *Home to Montana*, *Bison in the Killing Fields*, and *Women, War, and Work* (co-produced with his wife Dr. Victoria O'Donnell).

ISBN 0-275-96057-9

90000>

HARDCOVER BAR CODE